THE PAINTED BANQUET

THE
PAINTED
BANQUET

MY LIFE AND LOVES
JOCELYN RICKARDS

WEIDENFELD AND NICOLSON
LONDON

First published in Great Britain in 1987 by
George Weidenfeld & Nicolson Limited,
91 Clapham High Street, London SW4 7TA

ISBN 0 297 79119 2

Printed in Great Britain at The Bath Press, Avon

Betwixt mine eye and heart a league is took,
And each doth good turns now unto the other,
When that mine eye is famish'd for a look,
Or heart in love with sighs himself doth smother;
With my love's picture then my eye doth feast,
And to the painted banquet bids my heart ...

Shakespeare, Sonnet XLVII

FOR
CLIVE DONNER

Once upon a time I married, and with an iron determination that the marriage would work, coupled with a scant belief in the reality of it, I made a kind of offering. I burned every letter and postcard from any man I had ever loved.

They seemed to have written a great many. But as I pitched another load into the cheerfully blazing zinc rubbish-bin I thought how natural it was they should have done so – they were mostly professional writers.

I found it impossible to re-open one envelope, unfold one page to re-read anything for therein lay floods of tears which would have doused the flames. Into the fire went the years of my life that, up until then, I had most valued.

But the sacrificial burning of those letters was to no avail. The marriage I made at that time was already splitting asunder when I first met Clive Donner, he an established film director and I a high-flying costume designer. He knew nothing about me except the evidence of my work that he had seen on the screen.

I had appeared in his office as an isolated and, to him, unknown woman. No hint of any other world I had inhabited was visible. I had manufactured for myself a carapace as impenetrable as armour. And it is because Clive has, over the years, removed it piece by piece, leaving me once more open and vulnerable, and able to be happy without my self-manufactured protection, that I wish to give him the pages that follow. They deal with that part of my life from which he was excluded.

Having made the decision to write an autobiography I consulted those I have loved: the photographer, the philosopher, the poet, the novelist and the playwright. None had any objections. I even had a letter saying 'Jocelyn, I'm not ashamed and I don't see why you should be. . . .' I am not.

ACKNOWLEDGEMENTS

I particularly wish to thank John Goodwin for editing the text of this book.

My grateful thanks also to Felicity Bryan for her invaluable help in showing me which road to follow, to Sonia McGuinness, who compiled the index and turned pages of illegible handwriting into meticulous typescript, and, above all, to Freddie Ayer for helping me proofread these pages.

J.R.

INTRODUCTION

I would never have been born if my mother had discovered she was pregnant early enough. In mid-menopause with two daughters already, one eighteen and one thirteen, she believed, with relief, that her child-rearing days were over. Her only worry was a thickening waistline; her doctor told her that she was six months pregnant. Two months later, in July 1924, I was born in Melbourne, premature and weedy, and handed over to a nanny and my eldest sister.

From the age of one to three, I can only recall brief, unrelated incidents, like being made to give my dummy a ceremonial burial – 'You're a big girl now and only babies need dummies' – and standing alone in the garden next to my almost newborn cousin in his pram and wondering how much pain that ugly, rubbery baby could stand. My chubby three-year-old fingers squeezed as hard as they could and he let out a satisfactory howl. When his mother came rushing into the garden, I was found gently rocking the pram, as I'd seen grown-ups do, the picture of innocent concern.

My passion for clothes was wakened at three. My beautiful god-mother sent me wonderful dresses from Paris. I can see them all as clearly as if they were still hanging in my wardrobe.

Sometimes Nanny, known as 'Nurnie' to me and as Myrtle Pretoria Moore to the rest of the world, left me to go and look after a pair of anaemic twins, who were fed on raw minced liver and beef tea. I remember them always dressed in the palest pink crêpe-de-Chine with bonnets to match their dresses and complexions. I hated them for depriving me of Nurnie, whom I adored.

I was loved and indulged by my parents, who allowed me a freedom my sisters had never known, partly because my mother was now bored with children, and by the time I was six or seven she would talk to me as an equal. A solitary child, neither happy nor unhappy, I found it easier to relate to adults than to other children. It was only when I went to art school at fourteen, priggish and precocious, a sexual late-starter with a ferocious intellectual curiosity, that I discovered that every work-filled day was also pleasure-filled.

Art school in Sydney, where I stayed six years, was the first convict prison built in Australia, converted into a technical college. The long, oval cell blocks with their iron staircases and gantries remained untouched. The circular watch tower was the sculpture school and the painting school, where I studied, was a prefabricated studio with its own private garden.

Forty years later the college is still there, essentially the same, though the garden has been paved over, where once I used to lie on my back in the grass, under a fruit tree. Where convolvulous and wild roses once grew, the sandstone walls rise high and unadorned by anything except the broad arrows and numbers chiselled into them by those first English convicts, sent to the end of the earth for stealing a loaf of bread.

The end of the earth was not, for me then, an alien concept. It seemed to me that that was where I was. I knew I was growing up in a provincial city, which, despite its great physical beauty, left me silently screaming with claustrophobia.

Four years out of art school, I was thought of as a 'precious' painter of 'charm' whose work was mistakenly rooted in the reproductions seen in Phaidon Press books rather than in the vigour of the country where I lived. After my second one-man show – the preciosity sold quite well – I bought a one-way ticket to England. With paints, easels, my invaluable reference books, a wardrobe of stylish new-look clothes and £80 in cash, I set off on one of the first passenger ships to leave Australia for Europe after the war.

The ss Maloja had recently been converted back from a troop carrier to a passenger ship and it was still squalid. The cabin I shared with a friend was a windowless, airless cupboard in which five rats were trapped between Sydney and Perth. To this day I can still hear the snap of the trap, the squeal and the heavy thud as rat and trap fell from the bulkhead to the floor in the middle of the night.

I caught crabs from the swimming pool, and survived on a diet of boiled potatoes, not because nothing else was offered, but because nothing else was edible. In six weeks we had reached Marseilles. My patience was by then at an end. I left the ship and travelled across France to London by train, arriving at Victoria Station on 2 January 1949. I emerged on to the platform knowing that at twenty-four I had arrived where I wanted to be. London was huge and silent, covered in the first snow I had ever seen. It was the real beginning of my life, and the beginning of a love affair with England which has endured ever since. I was never for one second homesick for Australia, but I have never been able to leave England for any length of time without pining for it. Each time I return to Heathrow I want, like the Pope, to get on my knees and kiss the ground.

I am lucky. The life I have chosen to lead has given me the freedom to live it as I wished, to work how and where I pleased. I have also had the immense good fortune to love and to be loved. It is perhaps the men I have loved to whom I owe the most, the same men whose letters I burned one hot summer day in 1963.

I

During early childhood I went to a number of schools, the first a kind of progressive kindergarten, where we were encouraged to do collages, model in plasticine and make large, three-dimensional representations of the Nile Valley. We used blue tissue paper for water, sand for sand and rocky desert, and we made palm trees with painted leaves and plasticine trunks stiffened with wire so they didn't curl over in the damp heat of a hot Melbourne summer. But best of all, beside the blue tissue paper we would lay a thin layer of wet cotton wool on which we placed wheat. In a few days, with only a little watering from an eye-dropper, a straight green crop would grow on either side of the paper Nile. The pure magic of watching something grow capitvated me then for the first time. It was a pleasure which has remained with me ever since.

The kindergarten, called Oberwyl, had been the Alma Mater of my sisters, but by this time it had diminished into the most junior of schools. The two headmistresses, sisters, the Misses Garton, wore black skirts to their ankles and boned stand collars round their thin necks. They were frightening, and clearly lived in another era. The third sister, Miss Hattie, fat and jolly, a Rubens flanked by a pair of El Grecos, ran the school tuck shop, where for one penny you could buy a huge, dark chocolate gun with a delicious marshmallow centre, a chocolate frog or liquorice straps by the yard. I made one friend, called Meg, and together we later moved on to the senior school, St Michael's.

St Michael's, which I hated, was run by Church of England nuns, and the smell of Phenyle, used to disinfect the lavatories, became for me the odour of sanctity.

I had been there for about eighteen months when my mother noticed how amazingly quickly I wore out the knees of my stockings (which I insisted on wearing as I thought that plain black legs looked better with a short navy blue gym-slip than mottled flesh and socks).

'How do you pass your time, darling,' she asked, 'to wear out your stockings at such a rate?'

'On my knees praying,' I replied.

'What for?'

'Oh, it's not only me,' I assured her. 'We are all on our knees most of the day, praying for you, praying for Daddy, praying for the girls, praying for the school, then we say the Lord's Prayer and the Creed, and then we get up and sing hymns, and if we want to pray some more, we can go into the school chapel at lunch time.'

This saga of hours spent on my knees moved my whole family to activity. Telephone calls were made to Meg's mother, who had already decided that Meg and her elder sister were to be moved to Merton Hall, or Melbourne Girls' Grammar School, to give it its proper name. Its prospectus promised attractions quite incredible to me, 'art and musical appreciation' among them. My parents went to see the headmistress, an Englishwoman of great charm, Kathleen Gilman Jones. I was admitted to the senior school, reluctantly leaving Meg to the pleasures of 'art appreciation' in the junior school and the girls of St Michael's glued by their knees to the floor for most of the day.

Merton Hall was only a few minutes walk from home. Often I would walk back from school through the Botanical Gardens, supposed to be out of bounds to us, and meet Miss Gilman Jones, who, recognizing a budding fellow horticultural nut, would do no more than smile and say, 'Good afternoon, Jocelyn,' and pass on. No one ever suggested to me that I was flagrantly disobeying rules.

At last I was at a school where I was happy and time wasn't wasted. Even the tennis court at Merton Hall was special, being surrounded by a luxuriating passion-fruit vine. After a long game of tennis, we would slake our thirst by picking the hard purple fruit and sucking away at it as though it were nectar.

Life at home I enjoyed too. Our garden, though small, could have been landscaped by a student of Capability Brown, so careful was the arrangement of pale, fragile trees against dark, ponderous cypresses. There was a hedge twelve feet high of camellias in the winter and Ophelia roses in the summer, and grape vines and creepers of wistaria and jasmine climbed most vertical surfaces. At the far end of the garden was a T-shaped lily pond. Burnished goldfish lurked in its depths under lily pads, and on the edge sat all the neighbourhood cats, expectantly. Binker, my Sealyham, would banish them.

At one corner of the pond grew a rarity – a black lily of the Nile. The first member of the family to see its green spathe unfurled, revealing its almost black spadix, had to rush to pluck this from the centre of the flower, wearing rubber gloves and carrying a spade. We held our breath while the spadix, offensive-looking and smelling of rotting flesh, was interred. To leave it in the flower for even half an hour would compel every bluebottle in Melbourne to come to that one spot. 'Burying the spadix' was my first totally exciting experience in a garden. I felt as if I were concealing a murder.

My immediate family I loved in an offhand way, except for my father, with whom I was passionately in love. While still wearing my stockings out at St Michael's, the only prayer I ever uttered with sincerity and hope was that I should be allowed to die before he did. My memories of my father are not of a young man; he must have been in his early forties when I was born. He was tall and upright with a face like Scott Fitzgerald's, and his thick hair, brushed straight back from a high forehead, was dark with the beginning of silver streaks at the sides. His features were remarkably regular; a woman sculptor unknown to me once said his right and left profiles were perfectly matched – although I now doubt this. Still, there was a rare symmetry to his face, the eyes were a clear and miraculous grey, and his nose, which I envied with all my heart, was as straight as if ruled by a draughtsman. I inherited nothing of his physical appearance except the shape of my hands and perhaps my lips. His appearance was casually and rakishly presented, as though perhaps he didn't think about his clothes when, in fact, great care went into the choice of silk shirts with soft collars, large knotted ties, grey Homburgs and even black bowlers (a rarity in Australia). I like to think of him best in evening dress with a stiff wing collar, gold-backed white enamel and pearl studs and cuff links, and a monocle on a fine black cord, so that he could read menus or theatre programmes without disturbing the set of his jacket.

I suppose I remained in love with him until I was about fourteen. But he lingered on in my subconscious for much longer and for many years, in my dreams, lovers would suddenly turn into him. I remember with relief the first time a lover came and went without turning into my father.

Both my parents were beauties. At the time one never, or rarely, thinks about the sexuality of one's parents, but as I write this, I am aware that both my mother and father were objects of allure and desire to many of the people with whom they came in contact, she to much younger men, and he to much younger women.

My mother was small, about five feet two, with a mass of dark curling hair, big soft brown eyes and a nose that tilted at the end. When her hair started to go grey, it went in a band from side to side right across her head as though someone had picked up a paintbrush and painted it in about an inch from the front edge. She was a quiet, serene woman in repose, but also capable of great wit and gaiety, and she remained charmingly flirtatious until the day she died. There used to be a mound of yellowing press cuttings, which fascinated me, from the first fifteen years or so of their marriage, when they were both extremely glamorous creatures, she full of style in what to me seemed curiously shaped clothes with a chinchilla hat and muff or Poiret-influenced evening dress with aigrettes in her hair. She was not without vanity and I shall always remember her sitting with her chin raised in an extraordinarily regal fashion to prevent her neck from wrinkling.

My father was fourth generation Australian from purely English stock. His family owned grain ships until the whole fleet went down in a gale. As a child, he suffered from *petit mal* and had to be educated at home by governesses. Three of his brothers died within weeks of each other from 'galloping consumption', but he had a sister, Patti, who was the only one of any of my aunts or uncles who meant anything to me. Her house was full of family treasures, miniatures with dark frames and fading ink on the back saying 'de Ricàrds'. I was always told the family went back to William the Conqueror. God knows whether they believed it or not; I would have liked to, but didn't.

My father's parents lived to a vast age. My grandfather, Harry, was a fairly talented amateur artist and, when I first remember him, he had just had a leg amputated. He was eighty-three years old with only two more to live, so my memories of him are not particularly rich. My grandmother, Rosa Ellen, was an old bitch and well into her nineties when she died. She was English and yet another of those ramrod-backed women who looked exquisite, dressed in dove greys, beige and lavender. She didn't come to stay often, thank God, but once she pulled from her finger a thin gold ring set with three tiny pearls, three minute emeralds and one ruby, truly designed to the scale of a small hand. She called me over and said, 'Child, I would like you to have this. It was given to me when I was your age by my grandmother.' My mind boggled at its vast age and I carefully put it away until such time as I could wear it. 'Young ladies' didn't wear jewellery when I was nine. Many years later it was stolen with the rest of my jewellery by a Los Angeles thug.

My maternal grandparents were quite different. My grandfather, dead before I was born, was Viennese, from a family half-Catholic, half-Jewish. My grandmother was a Bavarian Protestant, rosy-cheeked and large. She and my mother used to speak German if they didn't want me to know what they were talking about. When she was dressed up, she was remarkably imposing, though she too seemed to live in the nineteenth century where clothes were concerned. Her skirts swept the floor and she was heavily corseted, swelling above and below the waist into generous curves.

My favourite part of her house was the kitchen and pantry, which had giant earthenware pans full of soused herring, jars of pickled cucumber, pastry cutters, jelly moulds like fanciful copper hats, and Delft and Dresden wall brackets. I was allowed to run around unchecked, making the lustres hanging from the red Bohemian glass tinkle. In the garden no one else's gardenias smelled so good in summer, and in the winter her daphne was bigger and sweeter than any other. The front veranda was like a fern grotto, full of maidenhair, staghorns, and New Zealand flax. You had to fight your way in past them.

My two sets of grandparents didn't like each other. When my father married my mother, the Rickards were up in arms; he was marrying beneath him, or so they thought. My mother used to tell a charming story of his proposal. She was a piano student, and most days he would meet her when school was over. One day, after a silence and standing with his back to her, he said, 'Will you marry me?' Without a second's hesitation, she said, 'Oh, yes,' and he fainted at her feet.

They were not blessed with their Christian names. My mother's name was Gertrud, and my father's was just plain Bertie after the hero of *Under Two Flags*, which Rosa Ellen had just finished reading at the time he was born. Bertie in a way is rather nice, and Gertrud isn't bad, but the combination of Bert and Gert is nothing short of disaster, and that's what they were stuck with for the rest of their lives.

The first eighteen years of their marriage were idyllic; no cloud appeared in the sky of their chic, sleek, gilded life, but with the advent of my birth, disaster hit, and hit with such a resounding crash that my father, who was an acute and intelligent businessman, was suddenly left isolated and bankrupt. Bad investments left him virtually penniless and my mother, who, like a Victorian woman, was kept cosseted and protected from the realities of money, found herself caring for a husband on whom she had always previously depended. He was in the throes of a nervous breakdown of such intensity that those unworldly doctors of 1924 referred to it as a brainstorm or brain-fever.

These early years of my own life are naturally hearsay, but his intention was to commit suicide. He walked upstairs to look at me sleeping in my cot, intending then to leave the house and shoot himself; but he looked at the small sleeping baby bundled in layers of baby-clothes and found he was incapable of so destructive a solution, walked downstairs again to my mother and, from that moment, started to rebuild his life with her help and that of my sisters. By the time I was eight or nine his debts were repaid. One sentence of my mother's is firmly fixed in my mind: 'Your father paid back every penny in the pound for each pound he owed.' What to this day I don't understand is how, when we were in severe financial straits, I had a nanny until I was three and I was in no way aware at any time that the quality of life was less than carefree; nor do I know why, from the very beginning, I was allowed to go to only expensive private schools, which must have been a severe financial strain.

Pauline, my eldest sister, still believed at the age of eighteen that babies came out of their mothers' navels, an advance but only a small one on gooseberry bushes. However, for her, I was a great joy, a real live, if rather undersized, doll and all the years of my childhood I remember both Pauline and Sheila playing with me or telling me endless stories which I grew to know so well I could say the words with them as I asked for 'The Twelve Dancing Princesses' for the umpteenth time.

Sheila, though younger, was the less soppy of the two and would beguile me into eating Brussels sprouts, which I hated, by telling me they were fairy cabbages. When I grew old enough to see my sisters with clear eyes, I observed that Pauline had an exotic, almost oriental beauty. Her features weren't regular, but her brow was clear and high, and her enormous eyes the same soft brown as my mother's; high cheekbones, exquisitely drawn lips and a firm, oval jawline. Her body was lean, in fact model-thin, and she used to be a photographic model of imported French clothes. She was still sitting on her hair when she was well over thirty and I made her cut it off.

Sheila was totally different. Her eyes were deep-set and dark, and her nose straight like my father's. Her neat shingled head was set with what one can only describe as accuracy on a slender neck, and her body, although tiny, was deliciously rounded and sexy, like a figure in a Watteau or Fragonard. Her moods would swing sharply, but not nearly as sharply as her witty tongue. Her life was not happy – she was reclusive and withdrawn, and felt that both Pauline and I were more gifted than she. This was a piece of self-deception which made her own difficult and quirky character acceptable to her, even if it continued to alienate other people.

Growing up with a much admired mother and sisters wasn't easy. From the age of eleven I can remember that the house always seemed full of people looking at me and saying, 'She's a nice child, but she'll never have her mother's or sisters' beauty.' I was painfully shy and had to be coaxed by my mother to enter a room with my head up, rather than looking fixedly at the toes of my shoes. That I should grow up at all was all I desired; I didn't care how I looked; all I wanted was to escape from the confines of childhood.

II

I was well settled into Merton Hall, enjoying learning, enjoying tennis and netball, and turning, I think, into a fairly well-adjusted child when, as the result of a handsome family inheritance, which needed my father's presence in New South Wales, the household was packed up to move to Sydney. My father and mother went ahead to search for a house, while my sisters and I followed by boat with Binker, who had the best days of her life, for her quarters were with the ship's butchers. She embarked snow-white and disembarked a rosy red from being patted by butchers' paws. She was given a bone that was as big as she to go to bed with, and at least three times a day was taken round the deck on her lead for a walk.

Sydney Harbour, so unlike Melbourne, was a revelation, something I had never imagined, a beautiful stretch of water with islands and inlets and gardens coming down to the sea. My parents had found a marvellous apartment in Elizabeth Bay, almost on the harbour shore. But with the arrival in Sydney of us three sisters, the family took on, in one sense, the character of gypsies: no sooner did we settle in one house, than another, even better one was found and moved into. In the space of twelve years, we moved from Elizabeth Bay to Bellevue Hill, from Bellevue Hill to Point Piper, from high up in Point Piper to lower down in Point Piper, which proved the perfect place with the whole of the harbour spread out beyond the garden. There we stayed, at least until I'd left Australia.

I made friends at my new school, Ascham, but from the point of view of learning, it was the worst possible time to change schools. Puberty is not an age when one is most secure, and I was suddenly

thrust into a whole new structure of learning, for Ascham's educational system was entirely different from Merton Hall's. This made
me resentful, because I knew my work was inadequate. My remedy
for this was to escape to the painting studio, where I always received a
welcome and no one ever asked me if perhaps I shouldn't be doing
something else. One term my examination results at French were
three out of a hundred, but the following term this bizarre figure rose
spectacularly to eighty-three, mainly because I was absolutely
determined to learn and had decided to work at it. History, geogra-
phy, and English grammer remained, however, total no-go areas. I
eventually gave up and started to try and enjoy myself. In my not
entirely successful pursuit of happiness I was too well mannered to be
open to the accusation of insolence, but insolence undoubtedly lay
beneath my attitude to almost everyone who taught me.

During the time I was not learning at Ascham, my sisters made
friends with Olga Penton, a self-consciously intellectual woman in
her late thirtes. She had black hair pulled tightly back, wore peasant
blouses with multi-coloured dirndl skirts, and looked like a Russell
Flint lady crossed with one painted by Norman Lindsay. The amber
beads around her neck and the gold bracelets on both wrists clicked
and jangled, and when she took up knitting it was like listening to a
percussion band. She introduced me to her husband with the idea that
he might like to take me sailing with him over the weekends. I think
the reality of this notion was to make an additional difficulty between
him and his very pretty mistress, who normally spent the weekends
with him; I was being used as an innocent pawn in their marital
games. However, Brian Penton was an astute, intelligent and witty
man. He was editor of the *Sydney Daily Express* and any game Olga
could play, he could play better. We made friends, and I would go
sailing most weekends with him, Norman Lindsay's son, Ray, and
one or other of Brian's colleagues. They treated me as a thinking
human, a near-adult, though I was not yet twelve, teased me and
taught me. What I wasn't learning at Ascham I learned over the
weekends spent with them. On my twelfth birthday, Brian gave me
his own large cedarwood paintbox, complete with brushes, Windsor
& Newton artists' colours, a palette and palette knives. I still have it,
albeit a bit battered with age. If anyone was responsible for pushing
me in the direction of painting, it was Brian.

The holocaust was drawing ever nearer, and relations of my

mother's from Germany and Austria were arriving in Australia one after the other. As people, I didn't particularly like them, but all that meant was that I found them socially hard-going and we had no mutual interest, or none I could discover.

At Ascham I enjoyed making friends, painting, playing tennis and badminton. Although Ascham was without religious bias, I suspected there was something wrong with a school of four hundred pupils only one of whom was Jewish and one Catholic. The school was simply a microcosm of middle-class Sydney society of the period. One way or another, I was fairly disenchanted. After two more years at Ascham, driving back one day to Sydney from a holiday in Melbourne I declared, 'I'm leaving school at the end of next term.'

My father kept his eyes on the road, while my mother slowly turned to face me in the back seat. 'Are you? What are you going to do?'

'I'm going to art school.'

'How often?'

'All day and every day.'

'Well, my dear, perhaps you are.'

I couldn't believe my luck.

I sat the examination for entrance to the art school of the East Sydney Technical College, and passed. There was only one large fly in the ointment; no student was admitted under the age of eighteen. My father, mother and eldest sister, Pauline, went to see the principal, Frank Medworth. My parents lent the proceedings their authority, my sister her silver tongue and knock-out beauty. The poor man ultimately gave his consent. I could start at the beginning of next term—aged fourteen and two days. Eureka!

The last term at Ascham limped past, but I played hookey from school to go to the de Basil Ballet. That brilliant company, descended from the great Diaghilev, was visiting Australia with Serge Lifar, Irina Baronova, Massine, Youskevitch and Danilova. I went to every matinée I could get into. I wasn't only seeing marvellous dancers but also at first hand the designs of de Chirico, Picasso, Bakst and Braque. Every minute away from school was the beginning of my real education.

At this time, two particular friends from school were Jan and June Williams. The Williams's house was always full and it was there for the first time that I met Alec Murray, who is still, fifty years later, a cornerstone in the structure of my life. He was twenty, tall, slim, elegant, and had come to Sydney from Adelaide to learn photography. The Murrays were an old family with old money and, with the exception of Alec, old-fashioned ideas. They all, save Alec, owned properties throughout South Australia. Alec's father, Douglas, had sold his station to enable him to join up in the First World War. Australian agriculturists were not just men of reserved occupation, they were by law forbidden to neglect their properties to join any of the services.

When Douglas Murray was an undergraduate at Cambridge, he met and married one of the very first English film stars, Madge Campbell, and triumphantly took her back to South Australia, where the fragile English beauty produced first a daughter, Molly, and later Alexander George Campbell. When Alec was two his father died as a result of war wounds and Madge Murray was left with two young children in a still unfamiliar land, so she packed them up and returned to England, found that she hated it, and yearning for the spaces and air of Australia, packed up once more and went back, this time to stay.

Alec's family were by no means poor, despite the fact that his uncle, Sir George, had left his entire estate of £600,000 to Adelaide University. To Alec, his favourite nephew, he bequeathed merely a gold hunter and watch chain, plus twelve dozen fine lawn handkerchiefs with hand-rolled edges and hand-embroidered monograms – they shared the same initials, A.G.C.M. There was no question of disputing the will, Sir George was Lord Chief Justice.

Alec and I formed a curious friendship; he used me like a microphone to pick up other people's conversation in crowded rooms, and for thirteen he found me strangely grown up, though I looked even younger than I was. We made an odd couple: the urbane young man with a ready wit and an enlightened but down-to-earth intelligence, and the almost silent, adolescent child with over-acute hearing. I used to stand and watch as Australian – can one call them debutantes? No! predators—fell over each other trying to engage his attention. But his manner was always reserved, even slightly critical.

An older girl than I, clearly taken by him, said to me one day, 'You do realize, Jocelyn, there are only two girls in Sydney well enough born to marry Alec?'

'Oh, yes?' I asked. 'Who?'

'Well me for one, and R. is the only other,' said she. I couldn't wait to tell Alec. One was an egomaniac, the other an even more raging nymphomaniac. His reply, when I recounted the story, was, 'Oh, the silly bitch.' In later years he was offered a million pounds by the father of the nymphomaniac to marry his daughter, but Alec politely refused.

My last day at Ascham, I walked down the long, winding gravel drive, took my panama hat off my head and spun it like a frisbee into the enormous rhododendron bushes that bordered either side.

Two days later I turned up at the art school. We were given our syllabus for the term: antique drawing, plant drawing, perspective, anatomy, lettering, life drawing, composition and painting.

During a lettering class, when I was fifteen, I was discovered by a courteous, silver-haired teacher writing in Gothic script with a broad-nibbed pen dipped in sepia ink: '*Le plaisir de l'amour ne dure pas, mais le chagrin de l'amour reste pour toujours*.' On a long page of handmade paper I had repeated it many times with a variety of experimental layouts and decorations. He stood silently behind me until he could stand it no longer. 'My God, Jocelyn, what sentiments to hold at your age,' he said. I turned and grinned and said I simply liked the sound of the sentence and the shapes it made.

For those first two years of art school I was treated with great suspicion by the staff. They would openly say to each other within my hearing, 'She won't be here long. With that background, you can't expect the staying power.' Or, later, when I'd learned to look older, 'She won't stay the course, she'll be off and marry as soon as she fancies someone.' In fact, I was the only student amongst those who started when I did, who not only stayed the course but stayed an extra year as well.

I was desperately embarrassed by the difference between my accent and everyone else's. My expensive schools had eliminated all Australian vowels from my speech. But by the time I reached my real aim, the painting studio, I was less self-conscious and there were so few of us, all sharing a common interest and vocabulary, that I didn't notice who spoke with what accent.

When Pauline was a child, my mother covered all the looking glasses with brown paper, as she was found posing in front of them in silent contemplation of her own beauty for hours on end. I don't think I ever looked in a mirror as a child, except to see if I'd parted my hair in the right place. It wasn't until sometime in my teens that I took a good long look at myself, discreetly used some of Pauline's make-up, borrowed a pair of diamanté hoop earrings and was both astonished and pleased at what I saw. Until then I had been unconscious of my appearance. Unmade-up and wearing a full, dark green corduroy skirt, fitted pink shirt and flat heels, my hair tied in a ponytail with a leather thong, I'd sailed through art school unaware that I was surrounded by Jocelyn Rickards clones. I used to pose for the life class so I knew my body was all right – I was simply a late developer, and it wasn't until wearing a green silk dress that I noticed my eyes were the same colour, that my lashes were long, and that the addition of my sister's earrings added a kind of unexpected sparkle to my face.

CHAPTER
III

I lived through the war almost without being touched by it. We suffered no shortages, and I don't remember being deprived of anything. One knitted balaclavas, posted food parcels, made camouflage nets, and listened to the news – but the fighting was taking place somewhere else. Life as an art student was carefree and the war impinged only twice on my consciousness: once when tiny Japanese kamikaze submarines were found in Sydney Harbour, and the second time when a shell exploded on Bondi Beach. The idea of danger was so improbable that I believed the latter was the thunder of a summer storm.

The classes I attended were very small, because almost the entire male student population was away fighting. I didn't notice. The war might have been arranged to ensure the high standard of my education. It was not that I was without sensibility, simply that I was cushioned against reality. It was all over by the time the catastrophic horrors through which other people had lived even dawned on me.

After my last year at art school I lived in Merioola, a large Victorian house, with other painters and sculptors, and Alec. We all thought and talked obsessively of the day when we would be free to leave Australia, and more and more our eyes were set on Europe.

By the time I arrived in London, a twenty-four-year-old girl, I had first-hand knowledge of only two aspects of living – loving and friendship. For five years I had loved and lived with Alec Murray, by now a brilliant professional photographer. Because of him I was able not only to travel hopefully but also to arrive successfully. He had set out six months earlier than I, staying in Adelaide for two or three weeks with his mother, *en route*. He knew he wouldn't be able to persuade her to visit him in Europe and was very uncertain when he would be able to afford to travel to see her again. From Adelaide he sent me a plea for twenty-four avocado pears, and from Perth, his last Australian port of call, a letter which ended 'Yours faithfully – so far.'

When at last I arrived on the platform of a wintery Victoria Station, Alec was there to meet me with an attendant group of itinerant Englishmen who had visited Australia after his departure; he had made a fine, ironic selection of those I had, in Sydney, glanced at, and more than glanced at. It was such an outrageously funny gesture that there was no time for even a second's uncertainty or insecurity. Alec and I just looked at each other and fell laughing into one another's arms.

He had been living for some time in Cranley Gardens in a large Victorian house owned by a Czechoslovakian refugee known as Dimi. When Alec was certain of my arrival, he took a room for me alongside his own already large, Biedermeier-furnished one.

We talked the first night almost entirely away, and finally flopped into bed in the small hours clasped in each other's arms like the Babes in the Wood. About nine-thirty the same morning, there was a gentle knock at the door. Alec turned over and I said, 'Come in.' In came an eccentric figure with a face scrubbed bright pink as with a Brillo pad and pale ears set at right angles to it. Dressed in an exotic sashed kimono, pyjama trousers and stout woollen socks, he carried a large mahogany butler's tray with coffee, toast, butter and marmalade for three. 'Hello,' he said, 'I'm John Deakin. I was too curious to wait another second, so I thought I'd make your breakfast.' He came and sat on the end of the bed and had breakfast with us, looking me over the while. Breakfast eaten, he announced, 'Well, I'm off to tell the others you're all right. They're curious too. Alec, why didn't you say she was pretty?' (Alec had never even said it to me.) 'I'm going to take lots of photographs of you.'

Like Alec, John Deakin was a photographer. He had just been sacked from *Vogue* because, in a moment of drunken excess, he had curtseyed to Cecil Beaton at the annual Condé Nast party. He lived in the basement, in a damp, glass-roofed conservatory hung with ancient olive-green plush curtains.

On the floor above us was Jenny, the nubile, sexy daughter of a country clergyman, who later achieved her ambition, married the millionaire of her choice, and was last seen emerging smothered in furs from a chauffeur-driven Rolls. Somewhere else was Mary, the sister of a well-known theatre designer, who'd run away from her middle-class family and public school to join a circus as a bare-back rider. Finally, under the eaves in the attic, were two young doctors of impeccable background who saved my sanity during my first spring onslaught of hay fever. Anti-histamines had recently been discovered and each night they would give me pills of different colours so that I could identify them and the effect they had on me. After trial and error, through a rainbow spectrum of capsules and pills large and small, I settled for a yellow one, which appeared to have no side-effects, eased my breathing and kept my nose dry, free at last from the waterfall I'd carried round in the middle of my face for weeks.

Easter 1949 produced a heatwave with temperatures rising into the eighties and I couldn't understand why anyone ever complained about the English climate – indeed, to this day I can't. To live in a climate where one season doesn't glide imperceptibly into another is for me a constantly recurring miracle.

As the baking summer of that year came to an end, we were joined in Cranley Gardens by our closest friends, Loudon Sainthill, the painter and theatre designer, and Harry Tatlock Miller. Harry, a writer, was born in Melbourne and went to school at Geelong Grammar. Because one of my cousins went there, I knew that sitting at a table on a raised dais in the dining hall and dressed in the school uniform were two life-size felt pigs. The pigs' table was set for luncheon or dinner, and if any of the boys misbehaved during a meal they were sent up to the dais to finish eating with the pigs. It was to this school that Prince Charles went for his Australian educational stint, but maybe the pigs had graduated by then.

It was after Harry had left Geelong Grammar that he and Loudon Sainthill first met. Loudon was born in 1919 in Hobart, Tasmania, but grew up from his very earliest years in Melbourne. He totally refused to go to school because he suffered from a severe stammer, which would get worse in unfamiliar circumstances: if he telephoned me and I answered, he would talk without difficulty; if anyone else answered, he became completely inarticulate. His lack of schooling left him free to teach himself by reading, and he became remarkably well educated.

19

When war came, Harry and Loudon were separated by the indifference of call-up papers and conscription, one going into the Navy and the other into the Army. Eventually, with the help of politicians, Governors and Governors-General, they were reunited as medical orderlies on a hospital ship, where they spent a horrendously gruelling war, but were at least together.

I first remember seeing Loudon in Kings Cross, the Soho of Sydney – still, though the war was over, in an army uniform, but one of his own devising. He was stunningly beautiful, with smooth skin like honey-coloured alabaster, tall, broad-shouldered and perfectly proportioned, his hair streaked a bit lighter with the sun. He'd adapted his uniform to consist of very sun-bleached shorts, cut a little shorter than the regulation model, a well-bleached khaki shirt with the sleeves rolled up, and those Gainsborough hats that all Australian troops serving in the tropics are issued with – brims down on one side and pinned up on the other with a regimental badge. An exhibition of his, 'A History of Costume Design from 4000 BC to 1945 AD', was then on at the Sydney National Gallery and it had an enormous impact on me, not so much for its accuracy of detail as for its wild flights of imagination.

Loudon grew up apart from his brother and sister, an isolated child without the friends he might have made at school and certainly without acquiring any knowledge of the homosexuality that existed in a wider world. All he knew was that he was unhappy. He found a girlfriend of whom he was fond and to whom he made love, but he was still unhappy: life didn't feel right and he didn't know what was wrong. His brother married, very young, a beautiful blonde Dietrich-like girl, so almost every day Loudon saw in front of him the possibility of a complete and loving relationship. Why did it elude him? Fortunately, at about this time, Harry entered his life, older, more worldly and infinitely more sophisticated. From their first meeting until Loudon's cruelly premature death at fifty they lived together.

The two rooms in Cranley Gardens for four oversized personalities proved two rooms too few, so we set about looking for somewhere else to live and eventually settled on a war-damaged house that we were able to take furnished for £5 a week, because we didn't mind sharing it with the builders who were dealing with the structural alterations and redecoration. It belonged to a woman called the Honourable Mrs Something-Something-Shuttleworth, much given to wearing trailing chiffon draperies and broad-brimmed hats. 'The House of the Sons of God – 666 Clareville Grove' was on a large brass plaque on the gatepost. Inside the house, if anyone leaned on a concealed light switch, a large silver paper collage portrait of her son (killed in the war) would be projected giant-sized on the ceiling.

It helped us to make a home in London that we had also lived together in Sydney in a very big late-Victorian house with a rambling garden. Alec had lived in the stable block and used the ballroom as a photographic studio, Harry and Loudon had had two rooms on the first floor in the front with windows overlooking the garden and the harbour, gleaming like a milky opal in the distance, and I had had a studio at the back with a view of the stables and vegetable gardens. When we were seriously saving money before sailing for England, fame and fortune, Alec gave up the stables and moved in with me. The rest of the house was peopled by painters and sculptors, and in some miraculous way we all managed to maintain sufficient privacy for us to work without intruding on each other.

The house, called Merioola, was owned by the Allen family. During the war, they still parked their electric brougham in the Merioola garage, putting its batteries on charge overnight. I would occasionally go out with one of the family in this elegant equipage. It had windows all round, solid rubber wheels, and two very comfortable buttoned swivel chairs side by side; totally silent, it was driven by a primitive sort of joy stick. It was the Allen family's acknowledgement of the fact that they regarded petrol rationing rather more seriously than anyone else. When Arthur Allen, the head of the family, died, Merioola was leased by an enterprising lady called Chica Edgeworth. When I first knew her, I suppose she was in her late thirties, a small, round, sunburned woman with elegant legs and feet, silver hair done in a chignon from which pink ribbons fluttered, slim hips and the most enormous tits that stuck out at right angles to her body. She built herself a small pink weatherboard office under a pepper tree in the back garden, and ran her upmarket rooming house with great style.

Looking back now, all of us who lived at Merioola were able to lead the most marvellously carefree existence at a time when the *mores* of Sydney society were nothing if not deeply conventional. We formed ourselves into a loosely-knit whole, and exhibited together as 'The Merioola Group'. Indeed, Merioola became Sydney's pet cultural zoo; we were fêted, shown off, indulged, and reams of rubbish were written about us daily in the proliferating gossip columns. There was nothing we could do that wasn't considered newsworthy. Our opinions were sought on any number of unsuitable subjects and, because we were very young and eager and endlessly self-assured, we all played out our roles, giving bravura performances. We also gave the best parties in Sydney, which was just as well as we had an absolute mania for party-giving, seizing on any excuse. We would decorate our studios with flowers and garlands, spotlight the coral and jacaranda trees at the end of the lawn, and throw open the whole house to our carefully chosen guests.

We had parties for the Ballet Rambert and their director, Marie Rambert, a flashing steel hummingbird who never drew breath and who, if one's eye strayed from her, would secure it again by turning cartwheels across the room. We had parties for six models from Paris who introduced the New Look to Australia, undulating down the catwalk like six Salammbôs, their waists cinched in by *guêpières*, their arses swinging gently like pendulums. They brought high style to Sydney, but a certain amount of anguish to me because Alec developed a *tendresse* for Carole, the most beautiful of them. I alternately cried and smiled until they'd returned to Paris.

Simply because we had a ballroom we gave balls; the Allen ancestors must have spun in their graves like tops; they'd had the ballroom specially built for the 1920 visit of the Prince of Wales. Unconcerned we danced until dawn. We also, once, used Alec's ballroom as a place for an Indian dancer and musician to give a recital. I recall standing and watching, between Claudio Arrau and Rafael Kubelik, my heart fluttering away like the feathers in the Indian costumes – for one look at Kubelik some weeks before and I, in my turn, had suffered a *coup de foudre*. Not long ago I met his Australian wife for the first time and she said, 'Oh, but I know you well, Rafael often talks of those young people he met in Sydney.' I said, 'Oh, my God, I was twenty-two.'

CHAPTER

IV

The tranquility that hovered over us at Merioola was not so easily attained in The House of the Sons of God at Clareville Grove, sw7. Merioola had been big enough for us to have privacy, and in any case we were busy and successful then. But in London only Alec was working, as fashion photographer for Odhams Press, and at the start he supported the rest of us. Harry had been an art critic for a Sydney paper, but was having difficult finding a niche in London. Although Loudon had exhibited at the Redfern Gallery before the war, when very young, he was taking time to establish himself. I was shattered by the new world I was in and discovering that it was far from easy to paint without commissions, though I was a good cook and den mother.

As a small boy Alec had met the Governor of South Australia, Sir Archibald Weigall, and his wife, and now, twenty-five years later in London, Gracie Weigall developed an old lady's crush on him. Born Miss Gracie Maple with millions for her dowry, she had married the epitome of an upper-class Englishman, Archibald Weigall, and was a figure straight out of an Evelyn Waugh novel. Curious about Alec's life in Clareville Grove, she invited all four of us for the weekend to her country house. It was large and comfortable, and as we arrived inside the front door, Gracie's elaborate gilt birdcage of a lift arrived on the ground floor and she, sitting in a small gilt wheelchair with curled gold wig to match, was pushed out by a footman.

After drinks and lunch, which Gracie constantly punctuated with, 'I must watch my diet, diabetes, you know,' as she crammed another spoonful of sugared raspberries into her mouth, we went for a walk in the garden. Gracie now transferred to an electric racing-wheelchair in which she managed the most circuitous garden paths without difficulty, revved her engine and drove over my left little toe saying gaily, 'My eyesight you know, very bad, affected by diabetes' – delicate evidence of her desire to incapacitate rather than to cripple me. Every time I left the room, she would turn to Harry or Loudon and say, 'I suppose Alec is rogering that girl?'

We had been asked to bring evening dress, and during Saturday's dinner we gathered that she was giving the staff Sunday off but had arranged a soirée on Sunday evening for the entire county, with a film, *Naughty Marietta*, and a buffet – to be prepared by us.

On Sunday afternoon she took us to the pantry. There were butter and eggs from the home farm and a larder stocked by Fortnum and Mason; she set us to work like the hired help. We just had time to bath and change before the guests were due. I kept complaining that it was naff to change on Sundays as I scrambled into an inherited, almost never worn, black satin Dior evening dress, knee-length in front, skimming the floor at the back, which miffed Gracie even if it didn't look better in her eyes than the neighbours' flowered chiffons and ruched taffetas.

When Monday morning came and with it the relief of leaving, we thanked her and kissed her goodbye. As we walked to Alec's car I noticed that Loudon, wearing his favourite generously cut plus-fours, was moving in a curiously stiff fashion. We left howling with pleasure as he unloaded the loot from his legs: Beluga caviar, tins of smoked salmon, pickled oysters and jars of superior olives. 'That'll t-t-teach the old b-bitch,' he stuttered with satisfaction.

While we were living at Clareville Grove, Harry and I little by little started to bring out the worst in each other. We sniped away like veteran guerilla fighters, God knows what over, anything, nothing. Fortunately, we recognized the bad aspects of our own characters and managed a state of armed neutrality until the lease came to an end and we were able to part without wrecking a friendship.

Harry and Loudon, were by this time both launched on paths to success, Loudon as a theatre designer and Harry as a director of the Redfern Gallery. They moved to a top-floor flat in South Audley Street over Constance Spry, a restaurant kitchen and Audrey Hepburn, still hoofing it in the chorus. Meanwhile, Alec and I moved to a flat in one of the first houses in Eaton Square to be converted into large apartments. We got it through luck and cheek. One of the architects doing the conversions had tipped us off that a large flat was going cheaply, because it had only one bathroom. Dressed with care – Alec wearing his great-uncle's watch chain, a black seal-lined overcoat slung casually across his shoulders, I wearing all the jewellery I hadn't sold for food – we presented ourselves at the landlord's door and announced we had no money but had to have a good address. Our effrontery worked. We were taken to 22 Eaton Square and shown a third-floor flat with a large drawing-room, three bedrooms, entrance hall, kitchen, one bathroom and separate lavatory, constant hot water, central heating and porter, all ours for £7 a week, to be decorated to our specifications. I remembered at that moment an evening I spent alone with my mother before I left Australia. We were gossiping about my eventual departure for England, and she said, 'I'll never worry about you because I'll know Alec's there.' She was clearly right to feel as she did. But then she added, 'But please don't marry him.' I was astonished, not so much because I believed the idea of marriage had never occurred to Alec, but that she should prefer to have her youngest daughter 'living in sin' rather than in wedlock. I asked why. She said, 'You've had the best years you can have together already – don't tie yourselves to each other.'

By the time we moved into Eaton Square, the strong ties we still had were loosening. We loved each other. We liked living together. Our loyalty to each other was indissoluble. And we shared everything except our beds. This had come about little by little, mainly I suppose because we were both young, with healthy sexual curiosity, and had started looking about at the inexhaustible attractions of London. Alec had by now left Odhams and was working successfully as a freelance photographer with a studio in South Kensington. Peter Williams, the ballet critic, had moved into the Eaton Square third bedroom, making up a successful *ménage*. Slowly, I had started working again after the culture shock of arriving in England, which had paralysed not only my hands but my brain, as though it had been poached and gone soft and soggy. With new-found strength of purpose, I was forcing myself to go to evening classes of life drawing at the Chelsea College of Art, simply to get my hand in again. I also did a whole series of paintings, some in ink and wash, others in oil, of Alec photographing models.

Then some time in 1950 through Alfred Hecht, that most distinguished of framers, I was asked by the Medici Gallery if I would
paint the front and back panels of a three-leaf screen they owned, a
very simple walnut moulding with an arched top to each panel and an
inset gilt slip. I leapt at the chance. The panels were about five feet
high and why I decided to use watercolour and Chinese white, instead
of oil, I cannot now imagine, but I did and the result was delicate and
fragile. On the front panels I painted three allegorical figures in a very
high-key grisaille on a terre-verte washed ground; they were draped
and pleated and decorated within every inch of their firm silhouettes.
On the back, I laid the same terre-verte ground and covered it with
hundreds of pale butterflies, some minute, some quite large, and all as
transparent and light as I could make them. As a result of this work
the Medici asked me if I would have a show there, so I set to for about
six months doing a whole series of drawings in ink, wash and Chinese
white. I had totally forgotten them until very recently when, visiting
my sister in Adelaide, I saw one hanging on the wall. I don't think I
could do the same sort of decorative painting now, even if my life
depended on it.

Before we left Clareville Grove and moved to Eaton Square, Alec
and I had been at a small New Year's Eve party given by a very pretty
lady of the theatre, Bunty McNaughton. 'I've asked an interesting
man', she said. 'You must take care of him. He won't know anyone.
All his friends are very grand.' I found myself looking after a small
man with a high forehead and dark curls. That he was an academic I
knew, because he was introduced as Professor Ayer, but what he was a
professor of I had no idea, as I'd only half listened to Bunty describing
him. As midnight struck I was standing alone on the staircase when he
appeared beside me, took me in his arms, wished me a Happy New
Year and gave me a long kiss. As Alec and I strolled home along the
Gloucester Road I said, 'I think I'm going to have trouble with that
little professor.'

When 'the little professor' and I lunched together a few days later I
found him engaging and witty. He encouraged me to order *artichaut
vinaigrette* because he wanted to see how I dealt with the discarded
leaves, and I had to ask him to repeat every sentence twice because his
speeded-up delivery was so different from the drawls I was used to
hearing. To him, I had no Australian accent. I'd been sent to schools
staffed by English teachers and the only giveaway was in certain word

endings: 'I've got a tickut in my pockut, Philup,' I am reported to have said to Philip Toynbee.

Initially, I was cautious. We dined together sometimes, he came to Clareville Grove for a drink, and I managed to keep out of his bed. After one particular meeting he said goodbye; he was going into purdah to finish some work. Three weeks of silence went by and, on my part, increasing irritability. I dialled his number. I said I was missing him. Within the space of an hour I was at his flat, 2 Whitehorse Street, over a tailor's shop and a bootmaker – not only in his flat but in his bed, bedded, and smiling all over my face. A few days later, when we were walking in Green Park together, I was so obviously happy that Freddie asked why I wasn't able to say I loved him. I laughed and said I loved him, but didn't think I wanted to get married. Oh, naïve Jocelyn, who ever mentioned marriage?

I was then still so innocent I believed that if two normal people fell in love, and there was no just cause or reason why not, they married. I regarded myself as abnormal for not wanting to do so. On his side, no man was ever more pleased to hear that I was not hell-bent on marriage.

When we met, Freddie was thirty-nine. Bit by bit – he wasn't at all secretive – I learned about his childhood, his early marriage, his first infidelity, his subsequent divorce and affairs. I learned about Renée, his ex-wife, who even after eight years apart from him still liked them to spend their wedding anniversaries together. They lunched together every Sunday. She constantly assured him, and he believed her, that she still lived her life for him and the children.

This capacity of Freddie's to accept people as they presented themselves to him is an aspect of his character I still find extraordinary. For a man of his intellectual curiosity it astonishes me that he never looks behind the façade held out for his inspection. Renée's façade was that of a do-gooding intellectual nun with some sort of interest in the social services. She was in fact a monster, who believed that I was a monster because I threatened her position as Mother Superior. We met only once, a grisly occasion at Whitehorse Street. We held our drinks uneasily while Renée, perched on the edge of her chair with her ankles crossed, kept leading Freddie conversationally down memory lane, smirking at me and saying, 'Of course this won't mean anything to you, but ...' I said very little and thought her irredeemably common, though Freddie assured me she was well-born. We hated one another on sight, which, on the whole, was lucky for Freddie. If we'd become friends, we could possibly have annihilated him – except that he's marvellously resilient.

The hurdle of my meeting Renée over and an acknowledged disaster, we continued our life, sometimes at Eaton Square but more often at Whitehorse Street. During the first year with Freddie, I was wary of meeting his friends. I liked the warm anonymous cocoon he wove round me and I didn't want to share with anyone else the time I spent with him. He was phenomenally gregarious, so if he went to a party I would meet him later or lie in his bed reading until he came home. I was also practising a form of deception. I found it amusing to be the brunette equivalent of a dumb blonde, because I had observed he was irritated by 'intellectual women'. He never realized that he was taking two of me out to dinner, the walking talking living doll, and the quiet thoughtful critical me whom I knew existed but he, as yet, did not.

After the Medici show, I started to do a lot of work in collaboration with John Siddley. He was a good and eclectic interior decorator with great flair and taste, and I enjoyed myself.

One morning he arrived early at Eaton Square, sat down and said, 'I have a problem, can you help?' He had been commissioned to do an entire house in, I think, Chester Row, one of those immensely desirable but tiny Belgravia houses where servants once rested their heads. His client, Maureen Swanson, was a brunette Rank contract star. Her dining-room was in the basement, looking onto a paved rear garden, and what she desired most in the world was eighteenth-century Chinese painted wallpaper, but was appalled when John told her how much it cost per inch, let alone by the yard. 'I thought', he said to me, 'you could paint birds and plants, oriental in feeling, if you cared to?'

I showed him some books of exquisite Chinese paintings full of peonies, poppies, bamboo, birds on the ground and in the sky. John said, 'Perfect. You might as well start straight away.' We made the five-minute journey round the corner. I was introduced to Maureen Swanson and to Dr Stephen Ward, the osteopath later involved with the Profumo scandal, who seemed to be acting as a production manager, co-ordinating builders, curtain-makers and paper-hangers. Down I went into the tiny dining-room and began to work. I laid a ground of typically Chinese neutral straw-biased green. My brush had wings. In two days the whole mural was planned, with white poppies bending in the wind, lotus lilies and peonies kept low to the bottom line, defined by a bamboo dado, and birds flying out of the plants into the sky, or resting. I looked at it with that real pleasure which doesn't usually come until afterwards. All the surfaces were wet, so I walked home to give them time to dry overnight. John rang me later; he'd slipped in to see it and was as pleased as I with the form it was taking.

Next morning, I turned up at nine and was looking at the walls deciding where to start work, when Stephen Ward appeared looking pink and discomfited.

'I'm afraid it's rather embarrassing, Miss Rickards. Miss Swanson says the walls don't look like wallpaper.'

I looked at him and at the walls. 'She's perfectly right, it's a mural and murals do not, of their very nature, look like wallpaper. Don't worry. She can hang as much wallpaper as she likes over what's there. Tell her I'm sorry not to have been able to produce wallpaper, but you need to be a machine to do that. As you can see, I'm not a machine. I'm a painter.'

I gathered my brushes and palette and put them into the cedarwood paintbox. As I said goodbye I thought poor bugger, what a job, little realizing of course that the problems of dealing with an uncertain star would be as nothing compared to the pathos and tragedy of the rest of his short life.

The next mural I did for John Siddley was for Jane and Jocelyn Stevens, and it was altogether more successful, except that I suffered from vertigo, and I had to paint it on a scaffolding over an immense stairwell. The whole time I was there, I suffered from morning, midday and afternoon sickness. Once it was so bad that I spent the day sitting on the edge of the scaffolding with my nose pressed against the mural while I painted veins on leaves that were so subtle they couldn't be seen from a distance of more than twelve inches.

During that first year the A. J. Ayer I knew and loved was Grote Professor of the Philosophy of Mind and Logic at University College London. His background was Eton, Oxford and the Welsh Guards, and he was the only soldier the British Army pronounced incapable of learning to drive. At the age of twenty-four he had written *Language, Truth and Logic*, which in its day turned English philosophy on its head. He loved teaching and gave his time and concern unstintingly to his pupils. But there were two Ayers (as there were two Jocelyns), the erudite professor of academic repute and fine literary style, and that other man whom Cyril Connolly called 'the London Freddyair', an urbane, charming hedonist, with dreadful underlying anxieties which emerged in his sleep when he would cry out, 'No, No, No,' or, as on one occasion, when he woke me singing in his sleep in a dirge-like voice, 'I'm always on the outside, on the outside always looking in.'

The only times he seemed entirely free from anxiety were when we were abroad; but the nearer the plane got to London Airport, the closer the black glums came until I used to imagine I could see Renée swooping through the sky on her broomstick.

Eventually, when it no longer mattered to me, Renée's umbilical cord was severed. All the years that she had supposedly been living only for Freddie and the children, she had been having a double slice of life for herself on the side: a distinguished socialist peer for weekdays, and Stuart Hampshire, whom she subsequently married, for weekends. Stuart Hampshire, another philosopher, seemed to enjoy placing his feet in Freddie's footsteps; when Freddie left London University for the chair in Logic at New College, Oxford, Stuart Hampshire took his position as Professor of Logic in London, and when Freddie withdrew his candidature, Stuart Hampshire took the opportunity to become Warden of Wadham College, Oxford.

To this day I'm not sure whether Freddie was the only person who didn't know of Renée's infidelities or whether he just wasn't willing to believe it, but he certainly didn't choose to know until Renée, in a state of menopausal hysteria over His Lordship's defection and marriage to someone else, broke down and confessed her unhappiness to him. She manipulated their lives until one of the men was swept from the board, at which point the whole game became like croquet in *Alice in Wonderland*.

During the first idyllic years with Freddie, weeks could go by without much trace of his black glums. I was very happy and became gradually absorbed into the fabric of his life. Early on he discovered there was no point in lying to me, and on the only occasion he ever tried to be evasive I had, as if by extra-sensory perception, an extremely vivid picture of what had actually happened. He had taken an old girlfriend out to dinner and at the end of the evening, mildly high and for old time's sake, they had tumbled into bed together. It wasn't important to either of them and I was only slightly piqued.

What I couldn't bear was Freddie not telling me. The whole episode had run like a film on a screen in my head, as had other episodes over the years not to do with Freddie, and once I'd convinced him that these movies-in-my-mind weren't figments of a jealous imagination but an unwanted attribute I possessed, he never again tried to deceive me.

His greatest weakness was an openness to flattery, a desire to be admired, above all by women. Sufficiently admired, he would coruscate and dazzle with his brilliance. In many ways physically, though not in his dress which has always been extremely conservative, he resembled the young Disraeli. I loved him with a single-minded devotion.

The first time I remember going to a large party with him was in the winter of 1950 at the I.C.A. in Dover Street. As we moved through the rooms we came upon a cluster of his friends. I was introduced and had barely said more than, 'How do you do,' when one of the women turned to Freddie and, not even *sotto voce*, said, 'I never have much liked your girls.' We ended the evening on a happier note at the French Club. This was a small club in St James's Street run by Olwen Vaughan, who also ran the London Film Society. She started the French Club during the war for the Free French, and it became popular not only with them, but with every writer, painter and film director in London. The food was basically French bourgeois, *saucissons de* Toulouse, *choucroûte garni*, good homemade pâtés, garlic sausage, and marvellous soups, all for what seemed like next to nothing.

The next bad reception I had was from the *Observer* critic and feature writer Philip Toynbee, normally the kindest of men, who for some muddled reason believed that I was a philosophy student on the make. But once that was sorted out, we became friends.

After those initial unwelcoming encounters I became a fixture in Freddie's social life, with an identity of my own. I ceased to be 'Freddie's girl' and became Jocelyn, the female part of Freddie who most nights could be discovered wrapped in his arms at the Gargoyle dancing to the music of the bandmaster, who would strike up *Oh, You Beautiful Doll* as we walked through the door. Freddie is the only man in my entire life I have ever been able to dance with. Our bodies moved together relaxed and unselfconscious in a single light-hearted rhythm. With everyone else I've remained as stiff and ungiving as a

31

poker. It was a great relief to me when it became fashionable to dance solo at some distance from one's partner.

The Gargoyle in those days belonged to David Tennant and seemed run solely for the painters and writers who made up our widening circle of friends. So many are now dead: the Scottish painters Robert Colquhoun and Robert Macbryde and the beautiful, sad, clown-faced artist Johnny Minton, generous and honest, of whom there is a small portrait by Lucien Freud, which even now makes me want to cry when I look at it. Lucien himself used to turn up at the Gargoyle with successive wives and girlfriends, each one like the dogs in *The Tinder Box*, with ever more enormous eyes.

Cyril and Barbara Connolly would go on to the Gargoyle after dining, as we did, at the Étoile. There, one evening, I remember Cyril pontificating at length about food. Barbara turned her head away, shook her lion's mane of hair, and said in her low carrying voice, 'I don't know how anyone who can't tell the difference between butter and margarine has any right to an opinion about food.'

Others had the courage to eat at the Gargoyle, but it required an absence of palate that we could never pretend to. So during those years with Freddie I was fed like a Strasbourg goose – at the Étoile, at a small Italian restaurant in Curzon Street which no longer exists, and at the White Tower. I still possess a tattered and kitchen-stained copy of Elizabeth David's *A Book of Mediterranean Food* that was given to me for Christmas 1951 by John Stais of the White Tower, with their own specialities stuck to the end papers. I don't know why I didn't grow huge.

The evenings at the Gargoyle began soberly enough with the writer Humphrey Slater playing chess in a corner, Philip Toynbee and Donald Maclean drinking and talking quietly at another table. But I would turn my head to Ruth Sheradski, my closest friend, and her lover William Sansom, the novelist, for only a minute, and turning back see Humphrey, Philip and Donald laid out cold like fish on a slab.

Sometimes we would spend weekends out of London with friends in the country. During a weekend with Joan and Solly Zuckerman, who was then Professor of Anatomy of Birmingham University, I learned, while playing bumble-puppy in their large leafy garden, that Freddie even played children's games to win. I play for exercise and without any sense of competition, so the outcome of each game was the same: Freddie won and I got no exercise.

Perhaps the time I most enjoyed was at Chiddingly in Sussex with Lee Miller and her husband Roland Penrose. All his life enthralled by painting, Roland was rich enough to indulge his passion. Their house was a treasure trove of Picassos and Braques, Max Ernsts and Magrittes. Roland had been a prime mover amongst the early Surrealists and a few of his own paintings also hung in the house. One I particularly remember was a portrait of his first wife, her face covered in butterflies, a bluebird nesting in her hair. In the garden there was a collection of modern sculpture, each piece sited in proportion to the surrounding trees. Once, while sitting in the garden on a summer's evening, the four of us drinking and talking, I glanced up and cried, 'Look, a balloon.' Sailing through the clear evening sky was an olive-green balloon with a basket underneath, and through binoculars we could see three bearded adventurers with maps and books, telescopes and compasses. As we watched, the balloon began to lose height. We scrambled into Roland's car and turned and twisted through the Sussex lanes until we arrived near an isolated wood where, with a noise of rushing and the rustling of leaves, the huge balloon came to rest halfway up a tree like some gigantic bird's nest. The bearded men with their maps and instruments emerged sullenly, and we went back to have a third drink before dinner.

Lee, once the most beautiful woman in Europe, had become famous as Man Ray's model and mistress, and as the heroine of Cocteau's early film *Le Sang d'un Poète*. She had spent the war photographing battle zones as an accredited war correspondent. She was, perhaps surprisingly, delighted by country living and pressed me into service, churning the butter in the morning and in the evening playing goose-girl. The geese hissed and spat as I tried to get them home with a large stick, used more in self-defence than to chivvy the angry birds to their beds.

Both Roland and Lee are dead now, and Robert Macbryde and John Minton committed suicide, so anxious to escape from living just at that point where their lives had scarcely begun.

Another place we stayed at was Stokke Farm in Wiltshire with Robin and Mary Campbell. Robert Kee, who had returned from his years as a prisoner of war nervous, shaky and curiously destructive, had sought peace to write in a tiny cottage on the estate. Mary's daughters, Nell and Serena, by the tycoon Philip Dunn, were living with their mother. Nell, a young, fair, Renoir beauty, was like a peach not quite ready for the plucking and is now a respected novelist and playwright. Serena, less loved and cosseted by Mary, was dark with gentle manners, and was later compensated for being overlooked by her mother; she married Jacob Rothschild.

Stokke was the coldest house I've ever stayed in. I remember thinking as I drank coffee stirred with a gold spoon that I would have preferred to stir my coffee with my finger, if they would only sell the spoons and heat the house. You could get chilblains on your way from the bedroom to the bathroom. Robin used to walk the long stone corridors in an angle-length Australian opossum coat, which I coveted more than any coat I've ever seen. When I asked him where he'd bought it, he said it had been acquired during the war against the long chill nights in the Western Desert. It's still my idea of the most glamorous and practical fur coat in the world.

Mary, like a chameleon, took on the colours of her current husband. I complained to Philip Toynbee at one stage that I sometimes found the atmosphere at Stokke more than I could stand, what with Robin attempting to be a painter and Mary as a consequence pretending to be an art critic. I was foolish enough to say this to him one Friday just as he was catching a train for a weekend at Stokke. He rang me apologetically on the Monday to say he was sorry but he'd been indiscreet, not to say treacherous. He'd passed the long train journey drinking and on arrival had said, 'Did you know Jocelyn dislikes you?' Robin and Mary were most surprised, he said, and really rather hurt. 'Oh, but I'm sorry, Jocelyn. I know I shouldn't have told them.' In fact, as the years went by, I became fond of Robin, although we rarely saw each other in later years. Eventually, Mary, who had been born Lady Mary St Clair-Erskine, tired of being a farming intellectual, married an American sporting journalist, and when that marriage too failed, she returned to London, Sir Philip Dunn and his millions. Meanwhile, Robin Campbell, by this time a respected figure in the Arts Council, had married Nell's great friend Susan, who was half his age and became a distinguished illustrator under her married name of Susan Campbell.

Often Freddie and I would spend the evening in St George's Square with Philip, Benedict Nicolson and Jocelyn Baines. Ben Nicolson was the elder son of Vita Sackville-West and Harold Nicolson, and Jocelyn Baines, much younger than both Philip and Ben, was at the beginning of a career in publishing. At the top of a veritable mountain of stone stairs they shared a large flat, living there during the week and all fleeing to different parts of the country at the weekend. Ben was a tall, gentle, very English man. I made the mistake of saying to him rather frivolously, 'Ben, I don't think you're homosexual at all; you *think* you are because of your parents.' His face lit up and he agreed that he too had doubts; he truly did love women. The next step he took resulted in a disastrous marriage.

It was at one of their weekly dinner parties that I dropped the carefully cultivated mask of Freddie's silent mistress. Philip was tossing back glass after glass of wine and Jocelyn Baines, who liked to play the part of an intellectual *agent provacateur*, was being provoking. I can't remember who the other guests were, but after half an hour's pretentious drivel I heard myself say, 'I've never listened to such a load of rubbish in my life.' Dead silence followed, and a look of total surprise on Freddie's face that I could have an opinion about anything other than painting. Ben suddenly said, 'Of course, Jocelyn, you are absolutely right.' I then had to defend my position. As I did so, I watched Freddie's face at first darting me warning glances, then reacting with disbelief – the doll could not only walk and talk, it was proving itself capable of thinking. From that moment I date the loss of innocent happiness in our relationship. Freddie no longer found total relaxation with me, though he still denies that this was the case.

Freddie's pleasure in his own achievements was almost childlike and, for the most part, very infectious. In 1951, during the Festival of Britain, both the Victoria and Albert Museum and the National Book League had exhibitions of the hundred best books ever published. Freddie, like Graham Greene, was represented in both collections, and as we went from South Kensington to Dover Street he kept telling me how lucky I was to be his chosen consort. By the time we arrived at the National Book League I was becoming irritable. Graham Greene, very tall and slightly stooped, was standing alone at the entrance to the exhibition as though trying to absent himself from his surroundings. He was there on the off-chance of collecting some friends to join him and ward off the boredom of dining alone with an expected Austrian visitor. Freddie plunged into the scrum of the party, abandoning me to Graham. Later we all dined together with Rose

Macaulay and the anonymous Austrian, and afterwards crammed into Rose's little car to go and look at the lights of the Festival Exhibition on the South Bank. Freddie didn't realize that not only did I like Graham Greene but also found him very attractive.

Initially, he and I were both tempted to toss our caps over the windmill, but neither of us wished to hurt the other people in our separate lives. We did, though, send Freddie a joint telegram to Mexico quoting the bawdy beginning of a poem by Rochester, giving him the page and line numbers should he care to look them up. Naturally, he hadn't included the *Complete Poems of Lord Rochester* in his luggage, thought our reference was to Mr Rochester in *Jane Eyre* and that we had both gone mad or, more probably, were tipsy, which to some extent we were. Graham still feels guilty at so thoughtless a gesture, but Freddie I think has forgotten it.

In 1953, when there was no more question of fidelity to Freddie and I was free to behave as I liked without any moral dilemma, I fell in love with Graham and he with me. But the timing for any long-term affair was wrong. I discovered though that even a short time as lovers can be, as it was with him, one of the strongest supports to an enduring friendship. An odd thing happened while we were together. I found I was seeing what he saw: he transformed London for me. It became a bleaker place than the more ornamental one I'd observed until then. That too endures. Sometimes I still find that I see something with Graham's eyes and not my own.

When Freddie was lecturing abroad, travelling to the heights of Cuzco and Machu Pichu, or going via Moscow to traverse China from North to South, Graham would take me under his wing. We went to the theatre and saw everything from Norman Wisdom in *Charlie's Aunt* to a sublime production of *King Lear* directed by Peter Brook with Paul Scofield as Lear, Diana Rigg as Cordelia, and those nastiest of all sisters, Goneril and Regan, played to the hilt by Irene Worth and Patience Collier.

During these years of close friendship, before Graham lived in France, I lost count of the platefuls of smoked salmon and the oysters and black velvet we had for lunch before walking to a cinema – which were then huge with big screens. Our taste in films was very catholic, ranging from *Carmen Jones* to *Julius Caesar*. Graham also taught me everything I know about the London music hall. With him I caught the tail-end of Collins Music Hall on Islington Green and the last night of The Granville, Walham Green, which was an occasion of tangibly potent nostalgia. Something uniquely English was dying, and there wasn't a dry eye in the house.

John Hayward, the scholar and bibliophile, was a close friend, independently, to Freddie, Graham and me. Stricken with multiple sclerosis while still at Cambridge, he had great courage. Though he was appallingly disabled in the middle of youth, health and high spirits, I never once, in all the years I knew him, heard him utter a word of complaint or self-pity. He conducted his life as closely as possible to normal. In a wheelchair, he worked at his immense, book-covered desk looking over the Thames, and in the evening made sorties into London literary life with the help of a porter in his block of flats, his French housekeeper and a firm of taxis. His flat, in Carlyle Mansions, was large, and for many years he had shared it with T.S. Eliot. When I went to have tea, we would often be joined by Mr Eliot, as I always called him. He in his turn, though never in my presence, used to refer to me as 'Pixie'. I remember him as a tall, shy, courteous man, whose eyes smiled before his lips. I never felt I was with a great poet (despite knowing he was), but rather with someone sympathetic and interesting who was totally unaware how attractive he was.

Graham enjoyed arranging treats for John Hayward, and they collaborated on the details. An evening which for no special reason was magic stays in my mind. Graham, John and I, with Mario Soldati, the Italian film director and novelist, went to Collins Music Hall, dining beforehand at Frascati's. John had chosen it to precede the show as the perfect *de l'époque* place with its trellises and potted palms, acres of starched damask, twinkling crystal and silver for an infinity of courses. Afterwards, tightly packed into a taxi, we went on to Collins, where we watched from the glass-enclosed bar, which made John's chair more manageable. I loved that bar. It is very curious and affecting to watch singing and dancing in total silence or conjurors conjuring without a word of their patter being heard. It's not quite the same on television with the sound turned down.

One summer Graham, who like me doesn't drive, hired a car and we went off to see an exhibition of Stanley Spencer's paintings in the village of Cookham, where he lived. Then I was impressed by Spencer as a painter, but not touched by him. Now I find myself recalling a painting, and wishing it were mine, of Christ in the desert with a scorpion in his hand. I still don't like the crowded paintings full of patterned people, but the simpler, more austere religious paintings I find extremely moving.

I used to argue with Graham about his religion, until one day it occurred to me that I was being impertinent and intrusive. I made a small speech of apology and vowed never to do it again. But I don't suppose it mattered. Graham saw me as a kind of happy savage whom he did not want changed. I once told him that I had had a constant stream of nuns to the door of Eaton Square.

'What for?' he asked.

'Begging for charity.'

'How much did you give them?' I told him. 'Beware,' Graham said. 'They have their methods of marking houses.'

On another occasion I had been reading Freud and said that out of curiosity I'd like to be analysed. 'Don't,' he said. 'Promise me you never will. You're all right now. You might never be again after analysis.'

Graham lived a very private life, and turned a wry eye on my involvement, through Freddie, in London literary life. But I was tremendously excited by it all – by meeting and getting to know people whose books I had read as an art student. I thought it a major miracle. My friendship with Graham has survived longer than those early dizzy acquaintances, which I soon realized were purely superficially glamorous. I was only too glad to discard them once I was seriously involved in work. Graham is not a man who is capable of a superficial relationship and as the years have passed, although we see each other less often because of geographical separation, our friendship has matured. I never see his writing on an envelope without my heart lifting and I find myself touching his writing with my lips and hoping he knows how very dearly I am attached to him. He is the only man about whom I've never held one vindictive thought.

I was working away at my own career during the days at Eaton Square, and film companies had started hiring my paintings to use as set decoration. Alec, going to see a film with Ingrid Bergman and Cary Grant, said to the friend he was with as an interior flashed on the screen, 'I know that painting, who's it by?'

'Jocelyn,' was the reply, 'and it's hanging on your wall.'

CHAPTER
V

A marvellous American model, Jane Sprague, who lived in Rome, arrived at Eaton Square with a letter of introduction to Alec. She had a mane of natural silver and gunmetal hair, and had come to London to have a badly botched nose job corrected by Sir Archibald McIndoe. She was very dry and funny, and had soon moved into the flat with us.

I shall always be grateful to her for showing me Rome. She would take my hand and make me shut my eyes until she had found the perfect position from which she could, like a conjuror, display to me an absolutely matchless view or object. My first sight of the Forum was her most spectacular triumph. We had climbed the steps to the Campodoglio, looked at Marcus Aurelius and Michelangelo's pavement, and then descended a narrow cobbled street, I having been told to keep my eyes on my feet. At a certain moment, we stopped and Jane told me to look. There below was the whole Forum gilded by the midday sun, a vision that has always remained with me.

Rome in the early 1950s was very much an English expatriate city, and all English actors who could speak Italian were at a premium, dubbing English films into Italian. With Jane as guide I came to know and love the city and feel familiar in it, so that whenever I have had to return there to work I would immediately be relaxed and happy. It was on that first visit that I saw the room from Augustus Caesar's wife Livia's summer villa which – miraculously preserved on its site, in all its freshness, by being filled for hundreds of years with fine white sand – had been removed wall by wall and rebuilt in the Museo Terme. I sat on a marble bench in the middle of it with tears welling in my eyes; it was like finding the Holy Grail. Suddenly what I had been searching for as a painter was spread out in front of me. I felt as though I were wandering in the Garden of Paradise through trees laden with fruit and alive with songbirds. The particular qualities that grabbed my imagination were the colours: melting cerulean and terre verte, Naples yellow, gold ochre, pale rose quartz pink, all used with such subtlety that, although I was almost convinced I was in a real garden, there was no depth to it; it was mysterious, but totally flat on the wall – something I was always trying to achieve.

Twice a year Alec would go to Paris to photograph the collections and, unless I was occupied doing something else, I would go with him. I found the lure of high fashion quite irresistible. My interest in it wasn't frivolous, it was passionate, and what I learned as Alec's photographic assistant proved invaluable later, when I became involved in the theatre and films.

This came about slowly and was entirely due to Loudon Sainthill. The first time I worked with him was in Sydney, when he was painting a front curtain for James Elroy Flecker's *Hassan* and needed some help in order to complete it on time. I'm told that, when I'd finished all the female figures, a painter, David Strachan, with whom I'd been at art school, stopped in front of the huge cloth, looked at it for five minutes and said, 'I see you've let that lady Leonardo paint self-portraits all over your design.'

But my introduction into films came after Loudon's first triumph as a theatre designer: the 1951 Stratford-upon-Avon production of *The Tempest* with Michael Redgrave as Prospero; Alan Badel, pale seafoam blue from head to toe, as Ariel; and the young Richard Burton as Ferdinand. The production was revived in 1952 and after the final performance its director Michael Benthall was concerned that it should not be lost forever.

With the help of Robert Helpman he tried to raise the money to get it set up as a movie. Loudon was asked to 'Mickey Mouse' it, which in plain English means to follow the script and produce a drawing for every cut of the film, long shot, medium shot and close-up. It's an immensely time-consuming and difficult task. Loudon started, and after three days' struggling produced just two drawings. There followed a beseeching telephone call, as a result of which, with a friend, Margaret Olley, today the very *grande dame* of Australian painters, I started the awesome task of reducing Shakespeare to comic-strip form. I can't remember how many hours and weeks we spent churning out endless postcard-size drawings, though I do remember that Margaret's fairies were much ballsier than mine and I had to redraw them. Eventually our work was mounted in large red-covered books, which I have never seen again, though occasionally a film company telephones and says, 'I have a series of drawings that are meant to be by Loudon Sainthill, but they look like yours,' and I wearily say yes – and think what a great pity it is that in the end no one ever turned that wonderful stage production, that beautifully designed fairy story, into a film.

No matter whether my relationship with Harry was loving or sniping, Loudon and I remained unchangingly loyal to each other, lovingly truthful and truthfully critical, and we were able to continue working together with the utmost pleasure.

Little by little I was beginning to gain more excitement from the collaboration necessary in design of all kinds than from the rather lonelier business of pure painting, and in the winter of 1954 I worked on Richard Buckle's Diaghilev Exhibition at Forbes House, London. I was given an empty room, three trunks of clothes, and told to get on with it – 'it' being to design the 'ambience' of a box at Covent Garden for the Royal Command Performance of 1911, an attic in Paris, the *plage* at Monte Carlo, and the figures to wear the clothes.

Undoing the clothes from their rustling wrappings of tissue paper was thrilling. First came the 1911 evening dresses of chiffon, lace and crêpe-de-Chine with inside each bodice two tiny sacks of sawdust discreetly to flatten any over-excited nipples. Next were the Poirets, looking like brilliantly coloured illustrations in *Le Gazette du Bon Ton*; and last of all, the sand and beige coloured Vionnets and Lanvins. Kathie McGill, a talented sculptor, made the figures of papier mâché over a base of chicken wire, and for each tableau we slightly exaggerated the period stance of the models. How she managed to do the work I'll never know, with nightly visits from a very engaging but very sloshed Brendan Behan. When everyone else was dropping, he'd arrive, a bottle in one hand and a newspaper in the other, his voice rising from the basement to the top floor, 'If you ever go across the sea to Ireland ... and watch the sun go down on Galway Bay.'

Once the figures were finished, the faces, arms and legs were painted flesh-colour and I applied make-up with a mixture of paint, rouge, eye shadow and lipstick. It was the first time I had conceived anything as a design rather than as a painting, the first time I had delegated some of my work to other people, and I found it all immensely satisfying.

The Diaghilev Exhibition, displayed in the rooms and galleries of what was, after all, just a very traditional Belgravia house, was an extraordinary success. It included changing lights and swelling music; a dressing-room with Nijinsky's actual *Spectre de la rose* costume over a chair; paintings as large as Picasso's front cloth for *Parade* and as small as a sanguine drawing of Ida Rubenstein as St Joan; a Sleeping Beauty perpetually on the point of being wakened by the Prince; and through all the rooms, large and small, wafted Diaghilev's favourite scent, Mitsouko. One wonders how he himself would have felt about the exhibition. Despite its exoticism it was in essence a very reverent tribute, and somehow, to me, the reverence contained too much English good taste and not enough wild and exuberant Russian theatricality.

By the end of 1952 Freddie and I had spent three happy years together, so that our friends, never content to let well alone, started to ask first one and then the other of us why we didn't marry. Even I, who had started out with no such intention, began to think it was a good idea. Freddie's morbid horror of being permanently caught, of losing his liberty, had a result that few could have foretold. His fidelity flew out the window, and a series of girls flew in. First I became a member of a duet, the week evenly portioned out between me and Miss x (Sundays continued to be kept free for Renée). Freddie, meanwhile, still innocently believed the evidence of the face turned towards him and did not see what lay behind it. I was without jealousy, he thought. In fact I was so jealous – so wildly jealous – that during the next two years I must have used up my lifespan of jealousy. That I was able to disguise it so that Freddie didn't notice is something I'm grateful for, as I believe it to be the most degrading and self-destructive of emotions.

Girls came and went, or came and stayed. Progressively I became part of a trio, a quartet, a quintet, and sextet (plus Renée). I didn't behave particularly badly, but I didn't behave well. Like an Indian tracker, I would leave signs for my rivals to read. Before I left Whitehorse Street in the morning, when the bed was already carefully made by Freddie's splendid Mrs Moore, I would go upstairs and wipe my finger across my freshly applied lipstick, turn the cover of the bed

42

down and smear my red tipped finger across the pillowslip. I would leave small reminders of my presence in the bathroom. And sometimes, feeling particularly malevolent, I would, when making love, scratch Freddie's back, so that the next pair of fingers could read by braille the story of my existence. This lifestyle, if such it can be called, was handled by Freddie with great dexterity. All the ladies knew about me, I knew about all of them, but none of them knew about each other.

It was when the sextet turned into a septet that I made a scene, simply because there were not enough days in the week. It wasn't the feeling of being pushed out that hurt so much. It was that I realized Freddie was fighting to the last ditch by fair means or foul against what had at one time appeared to be an inevitable marriage. He still had one trick up his sleeve, however, which neither my patience nor my knowledge of what lay behind it could overcome. With me, and only with me, he became impotent. If he so much wanted his freedom, I thought, it was better that he should have it. We never, then or after, went through a period of bitterness. There was no question of betrayal nor of my feeling betrayed. Freddie was simply incapable of behaving differently. I remained the most important person in his life for the next few years, but it was on very different terms. We became close friends, and so it is today, though less emotionally heightened.

Freddie, no longer under the pressures which forced him to take on a harem, simplified his life to some extent. We lunched and dined with each other regularly, and in 1956 spent six weeks together in Rome – Freddie working and I looking, with Jane, at all the things that by now had become old friends. That six weeks away from any other commitments either Freddie or I had was a last hope to sort out some kind of real life together. It didn't work, and I remember little else of what happened at that time in Rome except a dinner with e.e.cummings and Marion Moorhouse, his wife – of all Freddie's friends, the two I loved the most – during which cummings, trying to make me laugh, taught me four lines of ribald verse that, absurdly, have stayed in my mind:

> the mountaineers had shaggy ears
> and pistols in their breeches
> they banged their cocks against the rocks
> the craggy sons of bitches

43

A year or so into my changed relationship with Freddie, in 1955, Natasha Spender telephoned me to say that she had met, while lunching with Hamish Hamilton, 'an elderly American gentleman, a combination of courtesy and despair', for whom she planned to give a small dinner party as soon as Stephen returned from America. Were Alec and I free to go? She was inviting us because she knew we were both passionate admirers of his work. The guest of honour was Raymond Chandler. I have no idea what I expected him to be like, certainly not as I found him: medium-sized, squarish, carefully dressed and as sleek as a seal, the hair grey, the face a beiger version of grey, the eyes, as far as I could see behind his spectacles, grey also. The formality of his self-presentation, his Edwardian courtesy, seemed at odds both with every word he had written and with what Natasha had been able to glean of his life since the death of his wife, Cissie, some months before. In his despair he had tried to commit a 'neat' form of suicide by shooting himself under a running shower, to avoid making too much mess for the housekeeper. In the event, he missed, I suspect because his hand was shaky through his alcoholic intake, which by the time I met him was formidable.

He was a charming companion for dinner, but beneath the social accomplishments, the very old-world attitude to women, one was gloomily aware of his sadness. After dinner, Alec and I dropped him off at the Connaught and arranged to meet him again. Next day Natasha, who later wrote an excellent essay about this whole period of his life,* had a long talk with me about him. This sixty-seven-year-old man had touched our affections and we were concerned. It seemed he still leaned towards suicide as a means of escape from a life he found intolerable. We decided he should always have an engagement arranged for the future, because his sense of good manners would keep him alive to honour it. With Alec's help and that of one or two other devoted friends, we kept a roster of self-invited guests lunching and dining with him.

What, initially, we didn't realize we would have to deal with was his role-playing, his Philip Marlow persona: the tough American writer 'Set-'em-up-Joe, Give-me-one-for-my-Baby- and five-more-for-the road' game. Over one role, the Dying Man with 'cancer of the throat', I decided to call his bluff:

* *The World of Raymond Chandler*, edited by Miriam Gross, Weidenfeld & Nicolson

'Have you been thoroughly examined and pronounced inoperable?'

'No.'

'Well, I'm going to make an appointment with a very distinguished physician and you are going to keep it.'

'How do I know I'll be able to trust this quack?'

'This "quack" was personal physician to Queen Mary. If she could trust him, I'm certain you can.'

The appointment was kept. He was examined thoroughly under an anaesthetic and set free with the not altogether surprising news that he was suffering from chronic laryngitis and alcoholism.

He moved into a furnished flat on the other side of Eaton Square and all of us were always prepared to drop what we were doing at a second's notice and rush to his side. Alas, it was just the beginning of a gradual three-year decline down the slippery slope of anxiety, inability to work, overwhelming depressions spiced with Ballantyne's Whisky, that led to his death in 1959. I fortunately remember more of the good things, the extraordinary generosity, the wit and the intelligence.

I find myself increasingly wondering if Raymond was a virgin. His dedicated care for his mother, with whom he lived until she died of cancer when he was thirty-six, scarcely left him free to pursue a libidinous life, which anyway was alien to his nature. He cast women in heroically perfect moulds. Both Natasha Spender and I were placed on pedestals of such unscaleable height that neither of us could ever feel at ease there. In all the time we knew him no sexual demands of any kind whatsoever were made. True, when he'd polished off a bottle of Ballantyne's, his conversation became minimally racier, but then he was inhabiting a world of fantasy.

Two weeks after his mother died, he married Cissie, another mother, then fifty-four and eighteen years older than he. In the mid-1980s women may still be sexually active until they drop dead, but thirty years ago many mid- or post-menopausal ladies tended to forgo the pleasures of a sexual relationship. The fact that for periods of their marriage Raymond was alcoholic and Cissie ill makes the likelihood of sexual fulfilment even more remote. Another factor is that, engaging as he was, he was not an assured or attractive man. I wish for his own sake that he had been, and could have laid in rows girls like those in his novels.

In Frank McShane's biography I do remember he indicates that I
hurled myself into Raymond's arms and, if all other references to
possible affairs are as inaccurate, I am inclined to believe in my own
theory.

Later, in 1955, I lived in Rome for three or four months working
on a mural for Kenneth MacPherson, a man of intelligence and
independence whom I'd met with Graham Greene. He'd seen a small
painting of mine which Graham owned and asked if I would do a
mural for his bedroom. Graham's painting was no larger than six
inches by four and I thought Kenneth showed great courage in
trusting all four of his bedroom walls to me.

There are traces of Kenneth MacPherson in literary memoirs of
the 1920s, of his love affair with H.D. (Hilda Doolittle) and his
marriage to Bryher (Winifred Ellerman), the lesbian writer. And in
Peggy Guggenheim's *Out of This Century: Confessions of an Art
Addict* two chapters are devoted to Kenneth, but a Kenneth I never
knew – a spoiled, gilded youth. Of the Kenneth I did know, there is
no glimpse. He was indeed rich, and perhaps twenty years before I
met him he was like that, but I find it impossible to reconcile her
image of him with mine.

When I first knew him, he was in his fifties, tall with thick silvery
grey hair, very blue eyes, and a soft, soft voice. I found him a very
devoted friend and it was due to my carelessness and preoccupations
that I lost touch with him towards the end of his life. He had a
miraculous house in Capri, where he cared for the ageing and ailing
Norman Douglas. It looked over the Faragleoni and whenever
Graham lent us his own house in Anacapri, Kenneth was the first
person Alec and I would rush to see.

But Kenneth's bedroom, where I was to do the mural, was in his
apartment in Rome, in the Via del Babuino. Before I started thinking
of the design, he took me to every museum and Etruscan town
within a large radius of Rome – Tarquinia, Cerveteri and Veii. I
soaked myself in the haunting history of the Etruscans and the
marvellous gaiety of the paintings in their burial places. I had for a
long time been influenced by the Graeco-Roman paintings of land-
scapes, gardens full of birds, trees heavy with fruit, blues and greens
melting one into the other. They have an overwhelming feeling of
peace. But the Etruscans had more guts. Their paintings showed
clearly what they intended. Whereas the Romans diffused outline

and detail, the Etruscans were bold and strong, making statements rather than suggestions. It was this that Kenneth wanted, so I returned to London laden with Etruscan reference sources and settled down to design his bedroom walls. My designs for murals are always loose and flexible. I don't like squaring up the original design and transferring it to the walls, as I find this a mechanical device which kills all hope of the happy accident. Working with oil on paper, I experimented with a variety of ideas, keeping in mind the floor of the room, which was short strips of walnut wood treated with acid to turn it forever into a pure terre verte. Finally I was satisfied, so was Kenneth, and it was then a question of waiting for the builders to finish and leave the walls of porous plaster for me to paint on. As it turned out it was the happiest working assignment, thus far, of my life.

I took a small apartment in the Via Flavia – a studio with a kitchen and bathroom surrounded by a vast terrace – and every morning I would walk down the Via Flavia, cross the Via Veneto, go down the Via Due Macelle, up the Via Sistina, and then make a headlong rush down the Spanish Steps into the Babuino.

No one has ever worked under better conditions. Kenneth at one time had shared a gallery in New York with Peggy Guggenheim, and while having a drink before lunch I could either rest my eyes on Max Ernst's mysterious *Swamp Angel*, or hold in my hand a small silver Etruscan figure of a warrior, of whom I became so fond I eventually incorporated him into the mural. I was so totally absorbed by what I was doing that I was usually content most evenings merely to return to the Via Flavia and flop. However, I made friends with an Italian poet and documentary film-maker, Nelo Risi, who was married to Mitty, a talented, rich and impulsive girl with a superabundance of sexuality. She was someone I knew well. We had been both at school and art school together, and I had spent weekends and holidays with her in a large pink-washed house at Palm Beach on the Sydney coast. The house stood on a hill looking over the Pacific on one side and an estuary called Pittwater on the other. Alec came down for every weekend. I was then his friend and Mitty his mistress. Mitty believed she was ready for marriage, but, although Alec was very much in love with her, he doubted whether she was mature enough emotionally to take on what he believed should be a lifelong commitment. She had been born in America, so held dual nationality, and his suggestion

47

was that she should go to New York as a post-graduate student for six months and, if she still felt so positively about him at the end of that time, he would join her and marry her there.

While trying to decide what she would ultimately do, Mitty went to Melbourne to stay with friends. Within ten days she had met and married the foreign correspondent of a Melbourne newspaper and naturally, within three months, had regretted it. He was a nice, extremely intelligent man, but couldn't adequately cope with a spoiled grown-up child.

I was left to pick up the pieces and stick Alec together again, and it was when he had recovered that he didn't so much take my virginity as get it given to him. I was nineteen and it was an encumbrance I wanted to be without. Whenever I remember the occasion I laugh, because fortuitously I was wearing such an appropriate dress: white linen with a high round neck and long sleeves, the skirt embroidered with true lovers' knots. And, throughout the ceremony, as epithalamium the radio played the purest Mozart imaginable.

Freddie and I had been in Paris the day Mitty married Nelo Risi there, and I had met them again when I first went to Rome. By the time I was back in Rome painting the mural, the marriage was beginning to crack, and Mitty had gone off for a while with a friend of Nelo's, leaving him free, as she said, to take any woman to bed except me, for that would be *lèse majesté*. Not unnaturally the temptation proved too great for us both.

When I returned to London, Nelo and I kept up a desultory correspondence so that each knew what the other was doing. But I was beset by anxiety, for on my arrival at Eaton Square I was appalled to find Alec looking very thin and tired, and it look a great amount of nagging from me to get him to consult a doctor. Since the age of seven, when it was discovered he had inherited his grandmother's predisposition to diabetes, he had lived with daily injections of insulin. What he didn't know, and nor did I, was that if diabetics get run down and let it go on unchecked for long enough, their lungs become a willing host to tuberculosis. We finally discovered that this was what Alec was suffering from. On Christmas Eve 1955 he went into King's College Hospital, Camberwell, for what proved to be a sojourn of thirteen months. For the first three months they made him rest and eat. He had to lie without lifting his shoulders from the bed in order to help the lesion in his lung heal. With that amount of rest, of course it did, but only superficially, for as soon as he moved the wound opened up again.

The only solution was an operation, a very experimental one, not guaranteed to be successful, consisting of removing the diseased parts of the lung and filling the cavities with what looked like solid ping-pong balls with holes through the middle. The theory was that these allowed the lung to re-flate and became part of it as the healthy tissue grew through the hole in the middle. With Alec, this worked. Ever since I have had a profound respect for National Health medicine. I was more anxious and concerned over Alec's health than any other problem in my life. He behaved magnificently. I have never felt so much admiration for any man.

Sometime towards the end of 1955 Loudon, again finding he had taken on too much work, asked me to design the men's costumes for a period musical he was doing. I thought he'd gone mad. 'I've never worked in the theatre, Loudon; I don't know what's needed.'

'You know about clothes,' he said. 'I'll give you the period references and the colour of the sets. Of course you'll be able to do it.'

I agreed to try, read the script, and did about thirty drawings which I showed him. He looked through them very slowly, came to the end and said, 'I didn't realize they'd have such a strong personal identity. Now you'll have to do the women's as well.' He felt that the costumes should have a unity of conception, and if I'd done the men and he the women it would have been obvious to any perceptive audience that two different hands had been at work. And that was the real beginning of my working life as a theatre and film designer. In those days I was far more wilful than I later became. One actress, for instance, was superstitious and didn't want to wear green. I said, 'I'm sorry, but the choice is Mr Sainthill's and there's nothing I can do about it,' when, in fact, the choice had been mine. I was being obstinate because I thought I was right. Probably because I flew in the face of this deep-rooted theatrical superstition the show was a flop.

VI

Roger Furse, a distinguished designer of plays and films, asked me in early 1956 to be his assistant on a movie to be made with Laurence Olivier and Marilyn Monroe. I had first met Roger eight years before in Australia. He was there with the Old Vic Company who, headed by Olivier and Vivien Leigh, were doing a mammoth tour of *Richard III*, *The Skin of our Teeth* and *School for Scandal*, the latter providing the setting for an absurd mishap. Vivien Leigh, positioned behind a screen for the Screen Scene before the curtain for the act went up, had a fairly long time to stand doing nothing before she was revealed to the audience. So she would always take that day's airmail copy of the London *Times* with her, fold it into the neatest square imaginable and do the crossword puzzle, stuffing the newspaper down her bodice just before she was required to play the scene. But one night, by accident, an actor knocked the screen over while Vivien was still intent on ten down and fifteen across. She looked up at an audience hooting with laughter while she still held the newspaper and pencil in her hand.

Roger Furse had designed all three of Olivier's Shakespeare films: *Henry V*, *Richard III* and *Hamlet*, and their association in the theatre and in movies went back many years. The film he was now to design, *The Prince and the Showgirl*, had started life in the theatre, as a play by Terrence Rattigan called *The Sleeping Prince*, in which both Vivien Leigh and Laurence Olivier had starred. A fairy story about a central European prince in London for the 1911 Coronation who meets and falls in love with a chorus girl, it was a rather slight piece, but charming in the theatre due to Vivien's delicious playing of the girl. Marilyn Monroe was cast in Vivien's role in the film, and

Beatrice Dawson – known to her friends as Bumble – was designing Marilyn's and all the other women's clothes. Roger was responsible for the sets and the men's costumes.

For me, working with Roger was a godsend, because, with Alec in hospital and living on capital, it was essential that I earned some money. So for five months or a little longer my life consisted entirely of days spent at Pinewood and evenings rushing back to London to see Alec. It was my first real experience of a big-budget movie, and it was like being an observer at a civil war. Olivier and Monroe did not get on, and both stars had rival entourages of sickening sycophants who hadn't learned to say no and were like the ever-diminishing tails trailing behind comets. The amount of deceit and hypocrisy I witnessed daily as executives passed the buck from one to another left me open-mouthed with horror.

As well as doing the work normally expected by a designer of his assistant, I also, of necessity, had to be Roger's nanny. The alcoholic skids down which he finally slipped into some kind of nirvana on a Greek island were already well in place. All in all, it was the unhappiest film I have ever worked on.

I had missed out on the golden years of Pinewood, from the mid- to late 1940s – the years of Powell and Pressburger, Launder and Gilliat, David Lean and Olivier's *Hamlet* – and by 1956, though Pinewood still had good actors under contract, the studio didn't know what to do with them, apart from hanging huge publicity stills of them all the way from the door of the administration block to the restaurant. I don't remember any other noteworthy production going on while we were shooting *The Prince and the Showgirl*.

In addition to playing a starring role and directing the film, Olivier was also partly producing it, which was very nearly beyond the capacity of any single human being. As a consequence, his performance suffered, and what should have been lighter than a feather became literal and earthbound. Marilyn Monroe, the most insecure human being I have ever met, with a little girl's voice and a woman's body, was scared witless of him and he at no time did anything to reassure her. So the scene was set early on to deteriorate from bad to worse, which it inevitably did. Marilyn arrived on set later and later, sometimes disappearing for ages into the bathroom of her dressing-room, I suspect to stare into a mirror searching for someone she hoped she knew. On occasion Olivier would do as many as thirty takes on a sequence in which she had to say no more than a few words. He was a perfectionist, but it left her feeling misunderstood and lonely. What was so astounding was to see the rushes when this mysterious creature, scarcely noticeable normally, would dominate the screen as if lit from inside with electric light. The camera didn't just love her, it was obsessed with her.

Marilyn must have sensed that I was sympathetic towards her, because she was always friendly in a remote, dreamy sort of way, calling me 'Jarselin', and often when she would insist on having the set cleared of any superfluous members of the crew I was allowed to stay. In consequence I witnessed the shooting of a scene which added fuel to the already highly volatile feelings. It was a scene between Prince Laurence and Marilyn the chorus girl, which ended with her singing him a charming love song. Just before the camera started turning, Arthur Miller came on the set. He was standing in her eye line, so she sang the song directly to him without even a glance at Olivier, who was, quite naturally, incensed.

God knows whether she herself wished to project an image of such blazing sexuality. But I do remember Bumble bringing armfuls of wool jersey dresses for her to try on, all the right size, which Marilyn then changed to two sizes smaller. And even Bumble's cool cracked one evening when they were all going to a première together. Marilyn arrived at her house, where she was to dress, accompanied by Arthur Miller, in an enormous chauffeur-driven Rolls. Bumble put out her hands to remove the huge supple mink coat, and there before her stood Marilyn in nothing but a pair of high-heel sandals and fine black stockings.

The last day of shooting was like the last day of school, and after I had arranged a roster of hospital visitors for Alec, Freddie took me back to Rome.

I saw Mitty again. She had totally left Nelo Risi, or so it seemed, and was busily creating a new setting for herself on the island in the middle of the Tiber. Nelo and I tried to spend a night together, and humiliatingly failed because of Italian laws preventing people who hadn't all their documents with them from booking in to an hotel together. At the same time, Freddie was trying to charm a sensational blonde American girl into bed – and he failed too. It was a night of spectacular misjudgement on all our parts, and one of the most ludicrous misadventures in which I was ever involved.

Nevertheless, for me it was a much needed holiday, and Freddie had done some work, covering pages of foolscap paper with his miniscule writing, which looks as though a fly with wet feet has marched evenly from side to side across the page. We had enjoyed being with each other, but returning to London was sad. I knew it was the end of the line for him and me.

Back at Eaton Square, I was supported by a few close friends, among them Robin Fedden and Robert Kee. Robin, at one time Curator of Hughenden and later a distinguished member of the National Trust, was the author of a chillingly absorbing book, alas now out of print, called *Suicide*. We often propped each other up in times of need. A marvellously elegant man, he had a natural affinity with Alec. Sadly he is no longer alive. Robert, in those days, though a writer, hadn't yet become a uniquely intelligent interpreter of politics on television and the thinking woman's idol. I think both men genuinely cared about what happened to me, and they also provided a much-needed element of masculine clear-sightedness.

Then, to comfort me in a different way, there was Sonia Orwell, who started life as Sonia Brownell. As a young girl she had posed for William Coldstream and the rest of the Euston Road painters, and became known, to her own embarrassment, as 'The Euston Road Venus'. She worked as assistant to Cyril Connolly for years on the magazine *Horizon* and later worked with George Weidenfeld, when he first started publishing. She had an infallible eye for a good novel. It was she who rediscovered Jean Rhys and got her to finish, if my memory is accurate, *The Wide Sargasso Sea*. She married George Orwell when he was virtually on his deathbed, but neither of them realized it and were full of plans for a new and better life when he got out of hospital.

Sonia's way of consoling me for the loss of Freddie was to hammer home the message that all men are beasts, a view she held for no particular reason that I could fathom. I was inclined to take an equally gloomy, though different, attitude: that my life, at the age of thirty-two, had come to an end emotionally.

To put this assumption to the test, I spent two weeks of compulsive promiscuity, without desire and certainly without pleasure. Allowing myself to be bedded by at least seven men over fourteen days I emerged at the end of it with strong feelings of self-loathing, and for the next six months lived a life of nun-like chastity, which I rather enjoyed and found calming.

By this time a firm of textile manufacturers in Mount Street was paying me a consultancy fee to advise them on their window displays. With this and the amount I had saved from *The Prince and the Showgirl*, I didn't have to worry about money and was able to spend the rest of 1956 painting.

By the start of 1957, Alec was out of hospital and well enough to cover the French collections again. It was a marvellous, spirit-lifting return to work for him. I went with him to Paris and, once all the collections were over, I travelled down to Rome. Jane met me at the giant Termi di Roma, and bundled me into a pensione in the Via del Babuino, where we both clambered under the eiderdown and settled down for a long catching-up gossip. Half an hour later Nelo arrived and asked what I thought I was doing there when I could just as well stay with him. Jane unfolded herself from beneath the eiderdown to go and explain to the concierge that I would be moving to the Via Gregoriana, where Nelo had an apartment, austere and white like the cell of a scholarly monk, with enormous windows looking over Rome towards the Via Condotti and the Corso. The Via Gregoriana is in the part of Rome which I love best: two minutes' walk from the walled garden of the French Institute, where one could wander at leisure for hours or sit reading under a tree with the certain knowledge that no one would pick your pocket or pinch your bottom.

Nelo Risi was and is the most atypical Italian, much more of a Stendhalian Frenchman, ironic and witty. I knew when the affair started that it had to end in a matter of months: I was committed to return to London to work. But that didn't stop me entering into it with that totality that makes loving worth living; and we had both been bruised, he from Mitty's defection and I from fears of uncertainty. He didn't speak English and I only understood kitchen Italian, so we communicated in French, his – then – very much more idiomatic and fluent than mine. The pleasure of living under the same roof with Nelo, knowing that when he went out he would just as surely come home, had a healing effect on me after all the years of wondering where Freddie was and with whom.

I stayed in Italy for about four months. I met and liked Nelo's family. He and I went to Frascati together, to Pisa, where he was doing a documentary film on Galileo, to Santa Margarita and to San

Fruttuoso, the fishing village beyond the headland from Portofino, accessible only by boat, and approached by a harbour where fishing nets were strung up like scenic gauzes and the creamy pearly stone of the thirteenth-century abbey glimmered in the sun. Going into this remarkable church, where the Kings of Umbria were buried, was for me a chastening experience. The tiny congregation of fishermen's wives, their heads draped with black shawls, all turned to stare at the alien intruder, and I slunk out, seriously regretting my lack of faith.

From Santa Margarita I caught the train back to London, dark glasses on my nose to hide the fact that my eyes were often streaming with tears: I hadn't stayed with Nelo long enough to fall out of love with him. In a sense I have never fallen out of love with him (I sometimes wonder if I've ever fallen out of love with anyone), so that over the years, whenever we meet, at film festivals in Cannes or Venice, or fleetingly for a drink or a meal in Rome or in London, it always gives me a very special and particular pleasure.

VII

In 1958 Loudon Sainthill was designing the sets for a stage musical written by Wolf Mankowitz, *Expresso Bongo*, about the seedier aspects of show business, night-life, coffee bars and strip-clubs. He asked me to design the clothes. He felt – God knows why – that I was better able than he to judge what was worn in such situations. I didn't argue. I knew reference sources were easy to find, and above all I would be working by myself, only referring to Loudon for colour notes. I went to the first read-through of the play and made myself known to Oscar Lewenstein, who was producing it with Wolf Mankowitz.

'How will I know him?' I asked Loudon.

'You won't be able to make a mistake, he looks like a terminally ill Freddie Ayer.'

I went. The book was wittyish and, for me, the whole project was made infinitely worthwhile by the fact that the cast was led by Paul Scofield. Millicent Martin was, I think, playing her first starring part and Susan Hampshire her first part of any kind, one line as a deb in a nightclub scene, with which night after night she brought down the house.

I've forgotten what I was paid except that it was not much. Even so, to part with it caused Oscar great pain, only assuaged when the costumes, and indeed the whole show, received good notices.

I love working on musicals. You have to keep track of the dancers' movements so they won't be hampered by unmanageable costumes, and this need constantly to return to rehearsals makes for greater involvement. The cast was young and enthusiastic, and I was able to watch Paul develop his part, from his first tentative walk-through until the dress rehearsal, when he had delineated it all into a pattern of fine nuances.

Later in the same year I again worked with Oscar and Wolf, designing the costumes for a play by Jane Arden, *The Party*, with Charles Laughton, his wife Elsa Lanchester, Joyce Redman, Ann Lynne, and Albert Finney in his first West End part. I found the play whimsical, but enjoyed being challenged by the sheer self-inflated bulk of Charles Laughton's ego and Elsa's curious witch-like quality. Charles played an impoverished old man; but, despite the fact that he at once reduced all his suits to a state of utter depression, he never the less insisted on them all being made by his usual very grand tailors.

During rehearsals I used to lunch with Charles at Bianchi's in Greek Street and, as we walked from Shaftesbury Avenue through the Rupert Street market, the stallholders would call out to him: 'Nice to 'ave you back, Guv.' Their affectionate enthusiasm made me wonder if they or I had got him wrong.

The Royal Court Theatre under George Devine was at this time London's powerhouse of new writing. There, two years earlier, John Osborne's blazingly provocative play *Look Back in Anger*, directed by Tony Richardson, had spoken unforgettably for Osborne's own generation. Loudon and Tony Richardson had developed a close, creative working relationship, so that when it was decided to make a movie of *Look Back* Tony, as director of the film, asked Loudon to design a composite set for the main part of the shooting, the rest to be photographed on location at Stratford East, Dalston Junction, a cemetery that overlooked a canal, and a used-tyre dump.

I was anxious to work on a film which, unlike *The Prince and the Showgirl*, was made with love and guts rather than a crew of forelock-tugging yes-men. The main casting too was wonderful: Richard Burton, Mary Ure – John Osborne's wife of a year playing Jimmy Porter's wife, Alison, as she had in the play – Claire Bloom, Edith Evans. But my initial meeting with Tony Richardson was not encouraging. At a first night party, he was standing clapping to a drumbeat for limbo dancing, as the members of the cast went down on their backs and wriggled under a low stick without knocking it over. He caught my eye, beckoned and pointed to an empty space beside him. I went, but I don't think we exchanged a single word. I was aware only of how immensely tall he was. Loudon then invited us both to dinner, warning me sternly that if I wanted to help make the film I must not upset Tony.

I can't have done so, because I did work on it, and it was the beginning of a long and rewarding association.

Designing clothes or costumes for films is not a self-serving device to make the audience stop and wonder at the beauty of your invention; it is rather a means of conveying by a visual signpost the background of each character. If clothes are well designed, they are probably unnoticeable, but should carry within them a number of messages, like what kind of school the character went to, what newspapers he or she reads, what political affiliations he has, what his sexual inclinations are, whether or not his financial position is secure – and if insecure whether or not he cares. All this saves valuable minutes of screen time by getting points across through the eyes rather than verbally. The same rules apply to sets. Loudon made the only mistake I have ever known him make when set-dressing Jimmy and Alison's flat. Tony was worried by it and didn't know why, so asked me to go and see if I could find anything about it that disturbed me. The set, in fact, looked good, but Loudon had hung dozens of different, worn ties from every hook, handle and cupboard door. Jimmy Porter only wore one tie, a black one for mourning when he went to Ma Tanner's funeral. He didn't possess another.

Tony was directing his first feature film and won the support of the entire crew when he spoke to them on the first morning of shooting, explaining that he was a beginner and largely in their hands. I loved working with him. In those days he had the brutality of innocence, his rough corners hadn't been smoothed out, and although he was already a skilled manipulator, he hadn't developed the full Machiavellian techniques he later adopted, perhaps perforce to get his own way.

As the making of the *Look Back in Anger* movie was ending, Bermans, the theatrical costumiers, asked me if I would re-create Irene Sharaf's costumes for *West Side Story*. It was to be staged for the first time in London, but with an American cast. They would open in Manchester first and the clothes had to be made and finished merely from measurements supplied, but worse than this, Irene Sharaf's original costume designs had disappeared, and all Bermans had to go by were some not very good photographs with swatches of fabric stapled to them. Sitting in the wardrobe of *Look Back in Anger* with paper, pens, ink and watercolours, I drew from the photographs each character and his or her changes of costume, re-reading the script to make certain I was going in the right direction, and also hoping to God I

wasn't betraying Irene Sharaf's intention. In due time everything had
been made and checked against measurements and cast lists, and we set
off for Manchester: a huge entourage from Bermans headed by Harry
Schneider, a director of Bermans and their workroom head and chief
cutter, his assistant, me and the marvellous Maria whose fingers flew
like dragonflies.

The cast arrived the day after we did. The dancers came to try on their
costumes. Nothing fitted. Harry and I looked at each other, and
checked the cast list we had been given months before against the cast
list given to us when the whole production flew in that day. There lay
the error – Bermans had been given the measurements of the original
Broadway actors, most of whom had been replaced. That the show got
on as scheduled was almost entirely due to Bermans' dedicated work
through the three days and nights left to us before the opening. But as
the curtain rose in Manchester on the first night, I was sitting in a train
with a large drink in front of me. I'd seen enough during rehearsals and
there was nothing more I could do anyway. So I returned to London and
have never, thank God, been back to Manchester since.

At Christmas 1958, Alec and I, never full of Christmas spirit, decided
to escape it by going to Rome. Mary Ure and John Osborne, who felt
the same, came with us; also Mary Cunningham, who all those years
before had shared with me the horrors of six weeks on the s s *Maloja* on
the way from Australia to London. Mary and John seemed then a
marvellous golden couple: Mary superficially a fragile flower-like
creature, John thin and sunburned with very blue eyes. They had a
quality of a latter day Scott and Zelda Fitzgerald, young and glamorous. How serious a man John was I didn't at the time realize.

We all stayed at the Inghilterra in the Via Bocca dei Leone, which was
still then the nicest and least luxurious hotel in Rome. The weather was
mild and warm and we had lunch on Christmas Day at the Casino
Valadier in the Borghese Gardens with sleeves rolled up and dark
glasses on our noses. We went for drinks to Kenneth MacPherson who
had moved to a flat on the very periphery of the Forum which I envied
him more than ever. When he left his apartment on the Via del Babuino
he had persuaded the woman who had bought it not to wallpaper over
my mural, which she found too masculine, but to cover it with pleated
silk, so perhaps it's still there. I went alone to the Via Gregoriana to see
Nelo, and was overcome by nostalgia and tears, and when I got back to

the Inghilterra Mary Ure put me to bed with a sleeping pill, like a very efficient Scottish nanny.

Mary and John returned to London for New Year's Eve. Alec and I stayed on for a unique Roman ritual. Every piece of china cracked during the year is saved up for the stroke of midnight, then let fly from the housetops on to the heads of innocent passers-by. On 1 January 1959 we drove to the airport early in the morning over broken jugs, cups, chamber pots, plates, platters, and bowls.

During 1958 John Osborne had written a musical, an indictment of gossip columnists. Soon after my return from Rome, plans were made to stage it, and I was engaged as costume designer, with Kenneth McMillan as choreographer, Hugh Casson as set designer and Christopher Whelen as composer. The débâcle of *The World of Paul Slickey* is now part of the history of theatrical disasters, but everyone went into making it believing in it, and proud to be associated with it.

Mary at that time in early spring was at Stratford-upon-Avon, rehearsing Desdemona to Paul Robeson's Othello and Titania in *A Midsummer Night's Dream*. And as John and I worked together we drew closer and closer. Step by painful step we tried to ignore what was happening. I was very conscious of the possibility of betraying Mary's trust in me, although by now I knew her marriage to John was badly flawed.

Then fate took a hand. One evening after John, Kenneth and I had dined together and were sitting in John's house in Woodfall Street talking, the last real pea soup fog that I can remember settled on London out of nowhere. At about two in the morning, although John and I tried to persuade him not to, Kenneth groped his way out of the front door. I couldn't get a taxi. John said there was no way he was going to drive me. And I refused to walk.

When I went into Alec's bedroom in the morning, he was lying rigid with his eyes shut. He opened one eye, glared at me and said, 'Oh Jocelyn, you bloody fool.'

'Don't nag, Alec. I don't exactly feel full of wisdom, but no one's going to be hurt.'

There are things which flashed through my mind then that I wished I had said to Mary. I never imagined myself married to John, so didn't want to deprive her of a husband. Also I was six years older than he and he was not emotionally mature, so I knew that, no matter how much we were in love, I could never be the last love of his life. But I said nothing and events overtook us.

VIII

After the disastrous London opening of *Paul Slickey* on Wednesday 5 May, John and I got into his car and escaped abroad, little realizing that every gossip-columnist Paul Slickey was hot on our tails. Unknowingly, we escaped from them by travelling slowly along the secondary roads of France, stopping for a night or longer when we liked the look of a place. John, who when I first knew him drank only beer or whisky and was a nut-cutlet vegetarian, was gradually introduced to the pleasures of wine and the greedy gratification of French food. We stayed in Saulieu, where the great Maître Dumaine was still cooking at the Côte d'Or; we spent a night on the top of the world in a village called la Chaise Dieu, where we had a bedroom over the cows herded to sleep directly beneath us; and we holed up for almost a week in a village on the coast of the Camargue, where a storm raged, the sea was violent and the rain pelted down.

The village had a curious Tennessee Williams quality to it with a central canal lined on either side by run-down one-storey New Orleans architecture. We found a small, meticulously clean hotel open not only to sleep in, but also to eat in, and while the boats could still put to sea we feasted on bouillabaisse and fresh lobsters. From there we went along the coast of France to Italy, stopping the first night just over the border at San Remo, and the second night at Rapallo, arriving in the early evening at a baroque white wedding cake of an hotel where a nice hall porter, taking John's passport, said, 'Ah, the world of Paul *Sickly*', dived under the reception desk and came up with a scrapbook he'd been keeping of the Italian press notices of the play.

Next day we left Rapallo and headed for Rome, where we met Alec at the Inghilterra. He'd forgiven me, and all three of us were going to Capri together.

Alec was by now London photographer for *Paris-Match*, working for Ernestine Carter's fashion page on *The Sunday Times* and Serena Sinclair's on the *Daily Telegraph*, as well as being involved in the even bitchier world of the glossies, doing photographic features for *Queen*. So he was in a good position to hear the rumblings round Fleet Street. He told us horror stories of the vendetta against us in the English press, and produced cuttings. One, I remember, was a full-page article headed 'Would you let your wife or husband go away with another man or woman' and consisted of interviews with a variety of people, among whom Peter Brook emerged as one of the few who supported us.

Alec told us that Mary, in Stratford, was beset by reporters and valiantly carrying on. I'm sure she did it very well. I had learned from John that she was not altogether the forbearing, saint-like character she appeared. She was not above starting the day by hurling all the Copeland Spode breakfast china at him, leaving him in a sea of toast and tea leaves; and she could cry with the technique of an actor, all noise, but no tears. More importantly, in America just after their marriage in 1957, she had had an affair with an actor who was a close friend of John's and would regale John with tales which compared him unsatisfactorily to the American as a lover. John is incapable of feeling either sexual jealousy or sexual guilt, but he certainly felt betrayed. The American actor ultimately came out of the closet and is now as gay as a grig.

But before long, Mary, though denying it, was having an affair with Robert Shaw. It wasn't really surprising that her and John's marriage was floundering.

We drove along the autostrada to Naples with the hood down, and John for the first time let the car out. There was a very faint rain falling which heightened the scents of the countryside. I turned to Alec (a good driver but a bad passenger) and said, 'Isn't the wild thyme marvellous?'

'I don't know,' he said, 'we're travelling faster than the speed of smell.'

We spent the night in Naples at the Excelsior, which had a garage where we knew we could safely leave the car without the Jaguar engine being exchanged for that of a cinquecento, the cheapest

Italian car. Next day we crossed to Capri, and a friendly taxi took us up beyond Anacapri to the house Graham Greene had lent us. It was surrounded by a high white wall with an iron gate. We went in, locked the gate and felt safe.

Alec and I knew the house well, and had stayed there often. It's a place which calms the spirit and where life becomes deceptively simple. We remained there for weeks, lying in the sun, sitting on the terrace overlooking the Bay of Naples, and swimming from the rocks below Gracie Fields's swimming-pool, where Lucille Ball and Desi Arnaz would sit at a poolside card table and play poker from dawn to dusk.

Usually we lunched in a small restaurant next to one of the most ravishing churches I know, which stands in a square in Anacapri. While we sat on the restaurant terrace under the vines with an aperitif, a waiter would clamber up the hillside searching for wild *rugghetta* (arugula) for us. I had an unchanging lunch of salami, tomato and onion salad with or without *rugghetta*, and fruit. The patron, by then a friend of many years standing, looked at my hands one day, shook his head and said, 'Not married yet, Signora – you should give up the onions.'

An Italian friend, Nino Caprioglio, who worked as Alec's assistant on French and Italian assignments, had by now come to join us, and every evening the four of us would go down to the piazza in Capri for a drink before dinner. It was like sitting in the middle of a set for an opera. Enclosed on three and a half sides by the church and cafés, we would watch the laden porters trundle the luggage of the late arrivals across the square and down to the Gatto Bianco or the Quisisana. Occasionally a yacht would be moored at the Marina Grande and a load of high-living, whinnying English would trail across in full evening dress, preceded by their Greek shipowning host.

Alec's ears, as sensitive as radar equipment, could pick up the to him familiar click of a camera at fifty feet, and after our first experience of this in Capri, he made me walk along holding his hand instead of John's. The result was that back in London the newspapers received from their Italian stringers a fine collection of photographs of me affectionately with Alec – that is, until our last night when the four of us, strung out, ran for a taxi. I was leading, John following, and Nino and Alec bringing up the rear. At last the

paparazzi had got their pitiful scoop of the sinning lovers, two anonymous blobs running like hares and separated by a length.

We arrived back in London on an unreserved flight to find both
Eaton Square and Woodfall Street staked out with run-down reporters in raincoats. I escaped, but John was trapped in the cul-de-sac of
Woodfall Street, where a startlingly sexy photograph of him was
taken and printed in the next morning's paper. The telephone at
Eaton Square rang non-stop that day, congratulating me on having
been chosen by such a desirable man.

IX

John Osborne's second big stage success, *The Entertainer*, was first performed in 1957 at the Royal Court Theatre with Olivier's formidable performance as Archie Rice. By mid-1959 plans were well ahead to film it, scripted by John and Nigel Kneale. The director, as with the play, was Tony Richardson. I was designing the costumes.

The film, again with Olivier as Archie, was to be shot in Morecambe. Before starting on it, Tony was directing Vivien Leigh in Noël Coward's translation of a Feydeau farce, *Occupes-toi d'Amélie*. Called *Look After Lulu*, it was being tried out in Nottingham under Coward's pin-sharp eyes and laser-like tongue. John and I decided to go and see it there, and then leave early the next morning for Morecambe, where we could do a location recce for the new film.

Vivien was delicious in *Look After Lulu*, beautiful, witty, and also, when I went into her dressing-room after the performance, infinitely touching. Her marriage was on the rocks and she knew we would be meeting Olivier next day. She said she hoped he would see her performance. Noël Coward, overhearing our conversation, laid his index finger on the table, wagged it up and down, and said with irrefutable authority, 'Vivien, Larry has interfered with your career for years, there's no way he's going to interfere with this.'

In the hotel where John and I were staying we sat up till dawn drinking with Noël, who performed for us a private and scandalous autobiographical cabaret that remains a treasured memory. As we talked the night away I said, 'When I was an art student in Sydney during the war, you gave a Red Cross matinée and sang for the very first time *The Last Time I Saw Paris*; I've been yours since that moment.' He laughed with delight and gave me the day, the date, and the year. In fact, when anything was mentioned he would say, 'Ah, yes, the year of *Private Lives*, or of *This Year of Grace*', or whatever. He had in his mind his own calendar which wasn't marked by years, only productions. When I spoke, for example, of 1953 he would immediately say, '*The Apple Cart* at the Haymarket with Maggie.' He would sing us the verse of a song, gossip with wild indiscretion, and yet in no way did I feel I was with a man who was self-absorbed. As we went to bed John said, 'I thought you were a little forward rubbing your hand over his head.' I said, 'I loved him so much I couldn't resist it, and anyway I wanted to know how a crew cut would feel.'

In Morecambe next day we were met by Harry Saltzman, who was producing *The Entertainer*, and members of the production team and crew. We booked into an enormous comfortless hotel on the sea front, and then explored for possible locations, from Heysham Head with its mysterious rock-hewn burial sites, each one the size and shape of a coffin, to the other end of Morecambe Bay where, along the shingle beach, were Punch and Judy shows and donkey rides for children.

Later we planned to look at the local Palais de Danse, but first we returned to the hotel for dinner, which we ate at a long table, John and I on one side in the middle, Harry and Tony facing us on the other, with that dreadful hierarchical seating of union members, tailing off to chippies at either end. Tony started to talk about casting. Everyone working on a film has an opinion; if they don't, they should be in another job. Harry and John joined in, then Ossie Morris, the cinematographer, then I contributed something which I no longer remember. Tony suddenly whipped round his long snake-like neck and hissed at me, 'You're being employed to design the costumes, not to interfere in other areas.' There was a stunned silence. Eventually Harry said mildly that he thought my chief value was that I cared about everything.

Dinner drew to an uneasy close and we all trooped out of the restaurant, arranging to meet downstairs in ten minutes. My anger was contained until John and I reached our room. Then I said, 'You go, you must, but I'm not going. Nor am I going to work on the film.' John, concerned, agreed with me and was himself inclined to break from it.

When he got downstairs, Tony said to him, 'I had to stop Jocelyn.

She does go too far, you know. Don't you agree?' But as an attempt to drive a wedge between John and me it failed totally, and Tony came upstairs to haul me reluctantly out with the others. We went silently to the Palais, where one couple in a green subaqueous light were circling away towards the infinity of the ballroom's edge. I trod one measure with Ralph Brinton, the production designer.

In the morning we all caught an ungodly train back to London which zigzagged across England taking eight hours to do a five-hour journey. John and I, carrying every Sunday newspaper printed, found a compartment to ourselves. Tony looked in expecting that our anger at him would have evaporated with a night's sleep. When he discovered it hadn't, he said, 'You are *weeirrd*,' and shut the door on us again. Harry Saltzman also looked in, and stayed, worried not so much about the possibility of my not designing the film as about its contribution to John's disenchantment with the venture. Harry could see the whole film sliding out of the train window. He asked John to go with him to talk to Tony once we were in London. I thought John ought to go. His and Tony's working relationship had been long and successful. It would be foolish to throw all that away over whether or not I designed the costumes.

It seemed hours later when John came back to Eaton Square. Tony had been contrite and was sorry; he said he'd allowed his love for both of us to degenerate into jealousy, and had asked John to try to persuade me to continue working on the film. I said yes, but the whole experience was a very unhappy one. My friendship with Tony has always followed one extreme or another, so that we are either best friends or worst enemies.

Before the shooting started, Tony had tested and decided on Shirley Ann Field as the young beauty queen who becomes Archie Rice's bed-companion, Thora Hird as her marvellously shrill social-climbing mother, and Brenda de Banzie as Archie's put-upon and tearful wife. The remaining question was, who should play the important role of Jean, Archie's daughter? Tony and Olivier both wanted Joan Plowright – indeed everyone thought she was absolutely right. But Geraldine McEwan, though she was pregnant, was being considered too. There was a meeting between Tony, Harry Saltzman, Sir Michael Balcon – who represented British Lion's investment in the film – John and me to look at the rushes of Geraldine's and Joan's tests. Geraldine's situation was explained to Sir Michael. He thought and growled, growled and thought, and finally said, 'The other girl won't do.' There was a dreadful hush in the viewing theatre which seemed to go on forever. Rushing in where angels are too wise to tread I asked, 'Why are you against her, Sir Michael? She's a marvellous actress, will play well with Olivier and won't be intimidated by him – why not settle for her?' After John and I had left, Michael Balcon, apparently howling with pained rage, said to Harry, 'Who is that girl? Sack her this instant. I won't be spoken to like that by anyone.' Harry said, 'I'm sorry, Michael, she's important to us as the costume designer, and unsackable as she's John Osborne's mistress.' In the event Joan did play the part. But certainly not because I thought she was right; rather because everyone else – except Michael Balcon – thought so too.

John's house in Woodfall Street was tiny even by mews standards. Not only did he need a place where he and his secretary could work independently of each other, but one large enough for me to share, so he could be with me without intruding on life at Eaton Square. The perfect solution was found: a house in Lower Belgrave Street. The basement and ground floor were already taken, leaving us the first, second and third floors. A long narrow kitchen built out at the back had a terrace beyond, which in time, with a painted trellis round it and covered in climbing roses, honeysuckle and clematis, became a perfect flower-filled London garden. And I was within three minutes walk of Eaton Square, from which I had brought only paints, sketchbooks and easels, my clothes and reference books, but no paintings or furniture, as I couldn't bear the idea of leaving a physical gap behind me. At the time I didn't stop to think whether I was doing the right thing by leaving Alec; and even if I had, I shouldn't have acted differently. Alec and I could have gone on living together forever, but if we had, neither of us would have married; what we had was too much like the real thing.

I look back on Lower Belgrave Street with great happiness. John and I lived a life of intense privacy, and the house was light and airy, and we filled it with a mixture of modern and antique furniture. Alec was welcomed at any time – invited or not – and had his own special ring on the doorbell so that we wouldn't admit anyone else by mistake. My friend Barbara Skelton, by now divorced from both Cyril Connolly and George Weidenfeld, was also welcomed and used to come wearing what John called her 'shelter clothes': a pair of men's striped flannel pyjamas, a cashmere pullover covered by a djellabah and several shawls, thick woolly socks and fur-lined suede slippers, the lot topped off by a sheepskin-lined suede coat, and mittens. Like the character in N. F. Simpson's play *One-way Pendulum*, who was employed to come in and eat up leftovers, Barbara's first words every time she arrived were, 'My God I'm ravenous,' and she could be happily left in the kitchen for half an hour while she ate her way through the spare contents of the refrigerator. Most of my other friends I would see when John was away. He is a very shy man and I didn't want to inflict on him the residue of my life with Freddie.

Freddie rang and invited himself to lunch from time to time and John usually left us alone together. On one occasion Freddie arrived, had a drink before lunch and then, as we sat down to eat, launched himself rapidly, like a runner at the start of a race, into one of the most extraordinary speeches I have ever listened to.

'You know, my darling, I cannot behave as badly to anyone ever again as I behaved to you. It now seems very important to Dee that I should marry her, and so I shall – unless you wish to marry me?' To say I was dismayed is to underrate the strength and complexity of my feelings. I was deeply appalled that something I had so much wanted was now willingly offered, but obviously only as an escape from a marriage which he would feel obliged to celebrate unless I could offer him a way out. I put my head in my hands, tears streamed down my face, and all I could say was, 'But Freddie, it's too late.'

I had known Dee Wells all the years she had been playing out one of the roles in Freddie's life. When I got to know her I liked her, but the idea of a permanent liaison between them sounded like a marriage made in hell. And so it proved to be, with two mitigating factors: Freddie's friendship with Dee's daughter Gully – he was always better with children other than his own; and his pleasure when Dee produced their son, Nicholas. Their marriage ultimately ended in pain, acrimony and regret. Dee left London for New York with Hylan Booker, the larger share of the proceeds of the sale of the house in Regent's Park Terrace, where she had lived with Freddie, and most of the contents, Freddie keeping only family furniture, his books and a few paintings that were intensely personal.

Meanwhile Freddie and Vanessa Lawson, with whom he had long been having an affair, moved into a Georgian house in York Street. Vanessa, a great deal younger than Freddie, was one of the walking wounded after suffering through a long marriage to the Billy Bunterish Nigel Lawson. Astonishingly beautiful, like a small carved ivory Egyptian figure, she set herself to create an ambience where Freddie was able to work; she cosseted and cared for him in a way no other wife had ever done. He in turn loved and protected her, helped to rebuild her shattered confidence, and gave her the greatest gift it was in his possession to give, absolutely total fidelity. Eventually they were able to marry in 1983. They grew closer and evermore interdependent. It was one of the very few marriages I regarded as happy, but in July 1985, with no previous warning, Vanessa was found to have cancer of the liver and within six weeks she died with calm and courage, arranging her own funeral and sparing Freddie as much as she was able. There was surely a bad fairy present at Freddie's birth.

John very much wanted a child and with the help of obstetricians, gynaecologists, and a fertility specialist, I did at last manage to get pregnant, but at three months spontaneously aborted. John was in America. In my head I can still hear the doctor's telephone call to him from the foot of my bed where I was lying waiting for an ambulance, and unable to talk to him. I was taken to the only hospital I could be got into in an emergency, St Stephen's in the Fulham Road.

I'm not now sorry at what happened. I cannot think of myself as one of nature's mothers, and I suspect nature dealt kindly with me on that occasion. I wanted a child of John's, *for* John, because he wanted one so much. But I know it wouldn't have kept us together.

Of all the people with whom I've spent any part of my life, there is no doubt that John is the most complex. It is as though he uses the organs in his body for purposes other than those for which they are designed. He thinks with his heart, hates and loves with his brain, and creates with his emotions. In his work his emotions sometimes spill forth with bile and vituperation so lacerating and heated that I seem to feel my fingers burning as I turn the pages. He could be tender, concerned and loving one day and the next turn on Alec and me for being 'a pair of Colonial buccaneers', said with such searing, seething scorn that we wondered what in the name of God we'd done to call forth such fury. He's a man without hypocrisy, but sensitive to the pain he can cause by his unflinching attachment to

70

his own particular truths. He doesn't like to cause social embarrassment and will walk away from a situation that is likely to provoke it. The Jekyll-and-Hyde part of his character is most noticeable when the gentle man takes up his pen and uses it as a lethal weapon.

He still spent part of his time with Mary at Woodfall Street and the rest in Lower Belgrave Street. I suppose it was a compromise, but it didn't feel like one, and I had no wish that he should abandon Mary because of me. Then, simultaneously, two things occurred: Mary discovered she was pregnant by Robert Shaw, and an electrical fault caused the house in Woodfall Street to burn down while John and Mary were sleeping there. They were rescued unharmed by neighbours and the fire brigade. John drove Mary to one of those intensely conservative 'county' hotels near Buckingham Palace, and arrived at Lower Belgrave Street about five o'clock looking rather like a chimney sweep. Mary's pregnancy was by now advanced and an open secret. After a great deal of discussion about who should live where, Mary bought a house in Cliveden Place, though she still hovered round the edges of our lives. John, meanwhile, moved into Lower Belgrave Street, which was fast turning into a home for a formidable family. It housed not only us but also one short-haired miniature dachshund called Dolly, who was a veritable *reine de la Mafia*; a black-and-tan dachshund bitch named Walter after John's accountant; a very glamorous near Persian white alley cat, Fred, who had one clear blue eye and one yellow as a lemon; and a Siamese, Bert, who turned into my familiar. If I was feeling sad he would put his paws round my neck and gently stroke my face with his claws retracted.

Meanwhile Joan, John's secretary, was pregnant and anxious to give up work and get to the church on time. We advertised in *The Times* for a replacement and gratifyingly were inundated with replies. After the three of us had reduced them to a manageable number, and after the interviews had taken place, first with me and then with John, we decided in favour of Sonia McGuiness. Twenty-five years later she is still with me and typing this manuscript.

That winter John and I went to Portmeirion and took a cottage which looked over the estuary. Part of our reason for going was to try and find a country house for John. The sun shone as if it were midsummer, and it was so warm I swam in one of the sand declivities that form perfect chambré swimming-pools. The English newspapers were still tirelessly interested in us but everyone at Portmeirion was protective, and one day we were even lucky enough to hear this protectiveness in action. Two *Daily Express* reporters were talking to a gardener who was cleaning John's car under our windows. 'John Osborne? No there's no John Osborne here. Never heard of him. Ladies, what ladies? Lots of ladies in Portmeirion. They come and they go.' The reporters slunk off.

Living just outside Portmeirion were Rupert and Elizabeth Crawshay-Williams, he a graceful writer of philosophic memoirs. Elizabeth I hadn't then met but Rupert, a nice waffling intellectual, I'd known for years through Freddie Ayer, and they phoned to say that Bertrand Russell, who also lived locally, would very much like to meet John. Would we go and have a drink with them the following evening.

It became clear soon after we'd arrived that Elizabeth Crawshay-Williams was selfish and possessive to a degree, and regarded Russell as the gem at the top of the crown in her intellectual treasury. Russell's wife Edith was an American woman of Jamesian rectitude. Russell himself, a large whisky in his hand, sat in an easy chair by the fire and looked frail but still formidable. We were off to a sticky start, made worse because John was suddenly overwhelmed by shyness. He admired Russell, and his stand for nuclear disarmament, to such an extent that all his conversation dried up. I saw what was happening and moved out of my chair onto a cushion at Russell's feet, feeling like the dog on His Master's Voice labels. We had met in the past with Freddie, I reminded him, and we quite happily gossiped the rest of the evening away with cheerful indiscretion.

The next day I telephoned to thank Elizabeth. It was, I said, fascinating to have had such a long talk to Russell and a very great pleasure. She replied, 'Well, Jocelyn, Edith and I were amazed, because you must admit you have a very monotonous and boring voice and we wondered how Bertie managed to hear you.'

We returned to London without having found in Wales exactly the sort of house John wanted, so we continued the search in England, and eventually found a Georgian house-cum-watermill and granary in Sussex, the river Cuckmere looping through the garden. It needed a lot doing to it, but it seemed perfect.

Winter turned into spring and we became minimally more sociable. We saw Tony Richardson, George Devine, whom we both loved, and Jocelyn Herbert, the stage designer, who lived with him. George was a man I immediately felt comfortable with. Gentle, deceptively tweedy and pipe-smoking, he was I suppose something of a father figure for both Tony and John, certainly for John. He used to be able to control all the squabbling egos round a dinner table with the same authority with which he controlled the English Stage Company. My opinion professionally of Jocelyn Herbert swings like a weather vane. Her sets are very often wonderfully simple and effective, but I long for her to work with strong primary colours instead of the bleached bone and driftwood to which she is so addicted. Other old friends I continued to see either by myself or with John.

A new friendship we made at this time was with Roger and Penelope Gilliatt, he a tall saturnine neurologist, she a journalist for *Vogue* and then *Queen*. They lived in Lowndes Square in a flat which had nothing in it to displease the eye, for Penelope's decorative credo, like Syrie Maugham's, was based on white on white. Because her dinner parties were filled with visiting celebrities, and her food usually consisted of curling smoked salmon and watery scrambled eggs, we preferred to have them dine with us.

Little by little I watched Penelope, arrayed in a variety of unpressed azalea-coloured chiffon dresses, make a play for John. There was little

I could do *except* watch. Whenever he entered a room or spoke to her, she would light up like a one-armed bandit when someone hits the jackpot. Quite funny, though at the same time totally humourless, she was absolutely determined, come hell or high water, to secure John for herself. It was as pre-ordained as night following day.

I couldn't pretend that I didn't know what was going on. Her behaviour was too blatant. I had told John that I would not, indeed could not, be manoeuvred into leaving him; if any leaving were to be done it would not be done by me. I was still in love with him and had no feelings of pride, no matter how much the rest of me might hurt.

He and I had arranged with Tony Richardson to share a house in Valbonne in the South of France for the summer. I did say I would prefer to stay by myself in London, on the grounds that it would be more peaceful. But John responded by saying, 'I'm fed up with your mute attrition. I've been waiting for you to say that. Don't be so ridiculous, you need a holiday.' So reluctantly I agreed to go.

We set off in John's convertible Alvis, which had doors as heavy as Concorde's. Not far into France, the door to the passenger side broke and I was so busy holding it together with belts and dressing gown cords for the rest of the journey that I had very little time to think of anything else. There was no loitering on secondary roads this time. We drove as directly as possible to the south and arrived at La Baumette in Valbonne in the evening.

La Baumette was beautiful. Set among grape vines, olive trees, and a pinewood, it was an old stone farm house with the addition of a modern wing and a swimming-pool which, unlike most, was not an excrescence on the landscape but decently out of sight. The salon was a huge room with glass doors onto a terrace, where we ate all our meals shaded by overhanging trees. The property was looked after by Monsieur Voisin, who tended the olives and the vines, and turned the lavender hedge into the sweetest smelling oil of lavender I've ever held under my nose. His daughter cooked for us, and each morning, as though in an Edwardian household, she and I would 'do' the menus for the day.

Tony arrived; then Christopher Isherwood and his companion of many years, Don Bacchardy. I hadn't met Christopher Isherwood before, but because I'd read every one of his books and listened to stories about him from Natasha and Stephen Spender as well as from Tony, I felt I was being introduced to a friend. I loved his looks. He was small and nut-brown; his hair, a mixture of greenish brown and grey, was cut short, and underneath verandahs of spiky grey eyebrows were the most alive blue eyes I have ever seen. Don Bacchardy was younger and very beautiful with smooth brown skin and hair which then was black and is now prematurely silver. He is an artist of talent, with a very flowing line, a man of unalloyed sweetness. I would sometimes wake at six in the morning and before I went back to sleep would hear the two of them as they lay beside the swimming-pool in the early morning sun, one reading to the other: Don, with his exceptionally soft American voice, or Christopher with his harsher, more gravelly English tones which contained an occasional but marked American top note.

They were followed to La Baumette by others we knew, among them Jocelyn Herbert and her three children by her marriage to Anthony Lousada. We were a very full house. Every day a registered express letter would arrive for John from Penelope; every day I would have to sign for it and tip *le facteur*. John took to leaving them round the bedroom without their envelopes. I asked him not to as I had no intention of reading them. After that he carried them with him at all times, in a slim black briefcase. Tony asked me what was so precious to John that it never left his side. I replied, 'The Collected Letters of Mrs Gilliatt.' I do not think Penelope had confided in Tony because he looked astonished. On the other hand, she hadn't omitted to tell John that Tony had asked her to marry him.

While all this was going on Mary Ure was in a clinic in London giving birth to Robert Shaw's son. As a consequence, the trees which drooped over the terrace suddenly became alive with the sound of intrepid reporters alerted to what was happening. The telephone too started to ring, and ring, and ring. John always refused to speak. But one day, when I answered, it was an English journalist I knew by name, so feeling fed up I told him exactly what the reality was. He said his paper had suspected that that was the situation, but until someone verified it, they were obliged to keep on digging. He apologized for what we had been put through, assured me that they wouldn't be able to print anything I'd told him, and said he would arrange for a general dispersal. He kept his word. He was, if my memory is accurate, the permanent French correspondent for one of London's more reliable and upmarket newspapers, his name I have forgotten but I remember thinking as I spoke to him, thank God we have mutual friends, so he'll be predisposed to help.

However, no sooner did one turbulence subside than another blew up. Sonia McGuinness, all unknowing, rang me to say that the money John needed in Venice could be collected at such and such a bank. I put the telephone down and thought a bit. It was the time of the Venice Film Festival; Penelope was a film critic and would be there; so John was planning to join her. I walked slowly to the swimming-pool where John was and said, 'If you're going to Venice, you must talk to me.'

'I don't *have* to talk to anyone,' he replied and dived into the pool.

Eventually he did admit he was joining Penelope in Venice, but had only just decided to go, and Penelope had sent him the ticket. Would I promise to stay at Valbonne until he returned? I said yes, and off he went. Everyone at La Baumette, except Tony and Jocelyn, who now knew something of what was going on, was baffled. To the observer, John and I didn't seem to be on the point of splitting up, although, as Tony accurately pointed out, John's loves did tend to have a three- to four-year cycle.

Gradually the house emptied. Tony had to return temporarily to London, Christopher and Don left too; Jocelyn and her children departed *en masse*, and I then spent the bleakest week of my life, wandering round a large house which before had been bursting at the seams.

While in Valbonne John had written for *Tribune* a tremendously impassioned and notorious piece entitled 'Damn You England', and I felt it would be seen as an empty gesture if he didn't turn up at a vast CND meeting taking place the following weekend in Trafalgar Square. He had arrived back rather shakily from Venice, which had clearly been a resounding success, and when I suggested he should return to London for the meeting, he was relieved saying, 'Oh God, I did hope you would say that.' He seemed not to have resolved anything with Penelope and we spent a few days quite happily together. Then, leaving the car behind us, we caught a plane home from Nice. In the taxi from London Airport, as we approached Belgravia, John said, 'I'm going to behave badly again, my darling,' got out of the taxi, rushed into Chesham Place where Penelope now lived, and out of my life.

I was desperately unhappy, but had no intention of fighting to get him back. My only real regret is that at no time during our affair, not for a week, nor for a day, did I ever have him to myself without either Mary or Penelope standing as it were in the wings. I know there are elements in my personality that must have driven him mad, as there were times when he bored me stiff. But mostly I value the time we spent together and regard it now as a time when I eventually grew up.

The huge CND meeting in Trafalgar Square took place on a Sunday. John was arrested. Lower Belgrave Street, where I stayed on, was once more surrounded by journalists, who remained there most of the time for ten days. On the Friday, John, Penelope, Sonia Mc-Guinness and her husband Frank came to remove the contents of John's study – I'd been invited to absent myself for a couple of hours – and someone tipped off the Fleet Street papers of John and Penelope's journey hand in hand into a golden sunset – which meant to the Sussex watermill at Hellingly that John had bought.

As soon as he'd emptied his study, in fact the same night, I turned it into a workroom for me, so that it wouldn't be a gaping hole, like a mouth without a tooth. In such a short space of time did the character of the room change, that it was not an effort for me to go into it. The house and animals closed protectively about me.

John had said no when Penelope had suggested to him that I would find it too painful to live there and should return to Alec. It's true Alec did move in with me for a while, but mostly I was alone and didn't even answer the telephone. Christopher Isherwood got through the barriers I'd erected and came with Don to see me: 'Jocelyn, cry your heart out, don't try to be too brave, you'll leave a permanent scar if you do.' I took his advice and howled like a baby. It wasn't too difficult. I hadn't been able to eat for a week. Even a piece of dry toast or a water biscuit immediately made me throw up. I survived on small quantities of Fernet Branca, tranquillizers and sleeping pills. Alec spoke to the few friends I was prepared to see, and Ruth Sheradski with her coal black curly hair was asked if she were Penelope as she pushed her way through journalists to the front door. The journalists posted a note through my letter box saying: 'Can't we discuss this in a civilized manner?' Alec took them to the Plumbers Arms opposite, bought them a drink, and asked why they couldn't lay off me as I really hadn't done anything, newsworthy or not. They said their editors insisted they stay put until someone said something. I rang

John's solicitor, Oscar Beuselinck, and asked him to get John to make a statement. By now, I said, I had been housebound for ten days and one of the cats was missing.

John made a statement, saying that Mrs Gilliatt was staying with him and would be remaining for an indefinite time. The journalists withdrew, and that evening Fred, the white cat, who had been in an adjacent coal cellar for days, was returned by a neighbour to me more black than white and very frightened.

The finale to this little drama was provided by a telephone call from Mary Ure asking if she could come and look through the bookshelves in case John had left any of her books behind. She arrived with Tarn Bassett, Robert Stephens's ex-wife, a nice woman who was deeply embarrassed, and she and I made meaningless small talk while Mary went through hundreds of books, found two and carried them away. Loudon rang me later and said, 'What were you wearing when Mary came to see you?'

'A pair of cotton trousers and a brown cashmere V-necked pull-over, why?'

'She said you looked very "mistressy".'

Gradually I pulled myself together and started painting again. I did some large panels, like decorative botanical slices through land-scapes. Starting with the sky, they went down the trunks of trees, down the roots of plants, into water where fish swam among aqua-marine rocks. Birds soared towards the sun or landed on the water. If one of the landscape panels was the yellow and green of early spring, the next was the white and copper gold of winter sun.

While getting my hand in at painting again, I reflected from time to time on the aberration which makes two people fall in love with figments of their own imagination rather than the two people they find themselves living with. Penelope, I think, believed she could turn John into a gregarious, party-going, cliché-spouting, sub-culture intellectual. But she was, in fact, living with a very private and passionate man with strong likes and dislikes, which he was incap-able of changing for anyone. What he thought he was getting, I never asked.

Gradually we were able to see each other again. The pain was going, and I began to feel only pleasure when once more we spent time calmly talking together, which quite frequently we did. Eventually, when Penelope found she wasn't able to eradicate all trace of me from

John's life, she started to woo me, and John telephoned to say he didn't see any reason why I should agree, but Penelope would like me to spend the weekend in Sussex at Hellingly with them. I said yes, if Alec could come too. We drove down and spent a weekend so awful that I have almost successfully blocked it out. John from start to finish was speechless, encircled by a miasma of gloom. Penelope, who had also invited the director Mike Nichols, took no notice at all of what was disturbing John and behaved like a *House and Garden* hostess. Alec swallowed a cap from a front tooth. And Mike Nichols left on some pretext or other after sitting through, I think, one meal. Alec and I beat it back to London silent as stunned mullets.

The social threads I had let drop while living with John I now began to pick up. Then one evening when Lower Belgrave Street was filled with people, some of whom I'd never met, I suddenly felt a stranger in my own house. I left them all to it, went to bed, and resolved to change the pattern of my life.

For a start I acquired a French *au pair*. Jacqueline was twenty-eight and married to an industrial designer who was doing his *service militaire*. She had worked as a teacher with deprived and delinquent children for some years and was beginning to find it overwhelmingly depressing, so her husband thought she should do something constructive and learn English while he was away from Paris. She dropped into my lap two days after arriving in London. We were made for each other. My menagerie fell in love with her at first sight, and I was free of that feeling so difficult to overcome of wandering from room to room in a house which seems suddenly to have taken on a different, much larger scale. The very fact that someone was there when I woke up and went to bed, stopped the need to fill my time uselessly. I spent days at home working and reading. My French improved; I taught Jacqueline to cook. With single-minded dedication she looked after me, the animals, the garden and the house, which smelled of beeswax and flowers, and I grew absolutely devoted to her.

XI

One evening about this time I went to have a drink with Ruth Sher-adski. Amongst the people there was Leonard Rosoman, who had recently suffered an even worse blow to his *amour propre* than I. For thirteen years his mistress, Ginette Moreton-Evans, had promised, 'When the children grow up, I shall marry you.' The children had now grown up, whereupon she had changed her mind and decided to marry Robin Darwin.

I had known Leonard and Ginette ever since my arrival in England. Leonard I admired as a painter, and I found his extraordinary Christopher Robin looks attractive. Ginette I never liked.

Leonard was in a very low state: wounded, suffering, vindictive; and his state of mind was made the more painful because he was on the staff of the Royal College of Art where Robin Darwin was Provost. We fell into bed together for few reasons other than that we happened to be in the same situation, at the same time, and in the same place. We also knew each other quite well and each other's background, which cut out all the usual formal footwork at the beginning of an affair. Our interests too were reasonably similar. After a while I became pregnant. Leonard, being gentlemanly, wanted to marry me, but I couldn't see any reason why he should. As far as I was concerned, the conception could have been parthenogenetic, and I felt quite capable of dealing myself with what I regarded as *my* child.

This was the start of a period of serious bickering between us, and Leonard in the summer went to Italy while I lay with my feet up until the fourth month was safely past. The first evening he was back in London we went to Sadler's Wells to see Alban Berg's *Lulu* and had dinner afterwards. I returned to Lower Belgrave Street, and Leonard to Pembroke Studios. At six o'clock in the morning I woke up in mid-miscarriage and subsequently spent a week in the South London Hospital for Women.

Not too long after this drama, in early 1963, came an absolute godsend: an offer of interesting work that brought with it a necessary but, to me, dubious distinction. Harry Saltzman, by now in partnership with Cubby Broccoli, asked me to design the costumes for *From Russia With Love*, their second James Bond film, and overnight, due to Harry pushing my application at the right moment, I became a fully paid-up probationary member of the ACTT, or, to give this august sounding body its full title, the Association of Cinematograph, Television and Allied Technicians. The union had not been happy about my working on earlier films, and getting a screen credit, without belonging. In those days, with big movies, it was a case of no union card no job, or no job no union card – a vicious circle. Left to my own inclinations, I would have preferred not to be part of something that is closed shop. I joined because it was a practical thing to do from my point of view, for on big-budget films a producer can be placed in jeopardy for using non-union staff.

Terence Young directed *From Russia With Love*. Sean Connery was naturally and perfectly James Bond. Lottie Lenya, the widow of Kurt Weill, was Rosa Klebb, the Russian agent with a concealed knife in the toe of her boot; and Robert Shaw was the Russian agent who came to a bad end when Sean pushed his head out the window of the Orient Express as another train was passing in the opposite direction. The heroine was a remarkably shy and chaste Italian girl, with blonde hair, blue eyes and perfect skin, called Daniella Bianchi, who wouldn't, even when alone with me in the dressing-room, stand with her breasts bare. Harry came to me in a state of high excitement after watching rushes of one love scene between her and Sean. 'Jocelyn, it's not true what you say about Daniella. She is showing her nipples.' I showed him the blue chiffon nightdress she'd worn and said, 'Look, all rubber.'

The location shooting took place in Istanbul. On the way in from the airport we saw a man wearing weathered old clothes and leading a huge performing bear on a chain, followed by a pack of barefooted children, though the snow lay deep. When we later asked if we could film such a scene we were pointed firmly in the direction of the Hilton

Hotel. 'Turkey is a progressive country,' we were told. On the recce before shooting began, we sniffed our way through the heady spice market and stopped for lunch in a restaurant where we could still inhale the delicious fumes. Terence and I, unwisely as it turned out, had two plates each of exquisite tripe soup before separating – he to search for locations in a small boat, and I to do the same by car with the art department. It's difficult to say which of us had the worse afternoon – Terence, dragging his bare arse through the Bosphorous, or me without a blade of grass behind which I could conceal myself at all too regular intervals, as the tripe soup made its logical progress from entrance to exit.

In any event, Turkey proved a difficult country to film in with any degree of freedom and pleasure. The people are suspicious, the bureaucracy is appalling and, above all, the Turks are contemptuous of emancipated European women. Daniella and I used to be given an escort of ten stunt men when we walked from her caravan to the shooting location in the market place.

I went back to London ahead of the others to prepare the scenes they would shoot there. Whilst doing this my affair with Leonard continued in a desultory, squabbling kind of way until I'd had enough and some demon made me say, 'We must stop, and not see each other, or we must try, in which case we should marry.' Leonard went away to think about it, while judging the final year of the Scottish art schools, and on his return said yes, he thought we should marry. Two days before we did Alec came to see me and said, 'Just because you've said you will, you don't have to, you know. He'll bore you to death in three months.' My own attitude was that I was unlikely ever to fall in love again. I thought Leonard a good painter, and he made me laugh.

It was, as Alec predicted, a disastrous marriage, but one I in no way regret. For the first time since leaving Australia I'd done something active to change the course of my life. I could have gone on living at Lower Belgrave Street at John's expense for the rest of my existence, but now that I'd started working again, enjoying it, and making more than enough money to live on that didn't seem a very moral solution. God knows why it didn't occur to me just to take over the running expenses of Lower Belgrave Street. They were little enough and I could well have afforded it. Instead, I moved into Pembroke Studios with Leonard, and we grew to know and dislike each other.

There is no point in going on at length about a failed marriage. I behaved badly, though without feeling any guilt, and the only thing I can hold against Leonard is that, apart from painting, we had nothing in common. A divorce, for which I paid £25, seemed the best present I'd ever bought myself. The marriage had survived legally for seven years.

During those years I threw myself into designing with a whole-heartedness that had eluded me in the past. To escape from Leonard's presence and his fairly patronizing attitude towards my painting, I more and more immersed myself in working on any good film offered me. But even this met with his disapproval because I was making more money than he. I would find bills for the studio rent lying on his desk, remove them and send off a cheque (hearing no more until he requested the receipts for his income tax returns). Designing came easily to me and was something I could always fall back on to keep body and soul together, whereas painting I find a far more personal struggle and infinitely more fulfilling.

At this stage of our uneasy marriage I was only too happy to work again for Woodfall, this time with Oscar Lewenstein producing and Richard Lester directing *The Knack* by Ann Jellicoe. It had been a successful and sexy play, acted by a tiny cast, and was opened up to be a stylish, free-wheeling black and white film – the cameraman was David Watkin – full of visual invention and running gags, with a script by Charles Wood, and over sixty speaking parts. The principals were Rita Tushingham, Michael Crawford, Ray Brookes, and Donal Donnelly. With them was a delicious group of then relatively unknown long-legged girls, who memorably in one scene lolled on a staircase in striking uniforms of grey flannel and long-sleeved white knitted pullovers, and who later became stars of the international cinema. Jane Birkin, when she changed from grey flannel, wore a black rubber mac on a motor bike; Charlotte Rampling wriggled into a black wetsuit at the Ruislip Lido for a scene with Lucy Fleming where they waterskied in mid-winter. Jacqueline Bissett stayed in her uniform and Joanna Lumley looked sportif in white leather. No other black and white film, as far as I know, has ever been so scrupulously visually controlled: from Assheton Gorton's witty sets to all the costumes, nothing was used but black, white and a variety of greys. I had two weeks to prepare it in, which was a nightmare, but an enjoyable one. The main part we shot in a house in Shepherd's Bush, the rest at the Royal Albert Hall, in Mary Quant's Bazaar shop in Knightsbridge, at Victoria Station, and on the playing fields of St Paul's School. I remember one long tracking shot of Rita dancing down Kensington High Street shouting: 'Rape! Rape!', to which scarcely one passer-by gave even a passing glance. The swinging sixties were beginning to gather steam.

XII

In the early spring of 1965 Tony Richardson, by now married to Vanessa Redgrave, and with his reputation riding very high after the rich rewards heaped on the film of *Tom Jones*, which he had directed from an inventive script by John Osborne, said that Karel Reisz was going to ask me to design *Morgan – A Suitable Case for Treatment* as a starring vehicle for Vanessa, and he, Tony, was concerned that I should accept it. I was to do a film with Tony later in the year, *Mademoiselle*, from an original screenplay by Jean Genet to be shot in France and starring Jeanne Moreau. Tony, knowing I liked a long pre-production period, thought there might be a danger of my turning down *Morgan* if he didn't push me in the right direction. Vanessa had already had one child and was at this stage about eight-and-a-half-months pregnant with the second, and Tony felt she would need a designer who was also a close friend to support her through the early days of her first big cinematic role. Tony reassured me that there would be no conflict between the dates of *Morgan* and *Mademoiselle*.

Karel Reisz was a very different director from Tony, quiet and thoughtful and, when I met him, only ever comfortable in trousers three times too big for him. He would carefully consider the nuance of every mood and move. He had arrived in London from Czechoslovakia as a child, not quite in his teens, and from school he went to Oxford, where he wrote film criticism for, amongst other magazines, the important film publication *Sequence*.

Morgan had started life as a television play, a tragi-comedy by David Mercer, and the proposed film, with Vanessa, David Warner,

Irene Handl, Graham Crowden, Robert Stephens and Arthur Mullard, was in every way too alluring even to think of turning down.

In the event, designing for Vanessa was the sort of experience every designer dreams about. Very tall and perfectly proportioned, she had for me the sort of freshness that only someone who doesn't realize they are beautiful can possibly possess. God knows she's as blind as a bat, but even so I found it hard to believe that she and I could look at her in a full-length looking-glass and not both see the same flawless features. The first day, when I told her she didn't have to worry how she looked from any angle, she appeared quite stunned and myopically approached the mirror, put her glasses on and studied herself from head to toe. To be able to give someone an awareness of their own beauty is like giving them an amazing present. If they know that even only one person watching them is constantly doing so with pleasure, it transforms their attitude to themselves. I believe too that those who aren't beautiful can be taught to assume beauty at will if they are given enough confidence. But with Vanessa it was no illusion; she was the real thing, from hair to toenails and fingertips to fingertips.

Irene Handl and David Warner as widowed mother and son, both of them converted over the years to working-class Marxism (as opposed to the academic kind) by the dead husband/father, acted together like fine instrumentalists playing a duet. Irene Handl was a total revelation to me of the kind of hardworking character actress who leaves no detail of performance or appearance to chance. I went to see her not knowing what to expect and was ushered in by a maid to an extremely elegant drawing-room, everything in it chosen with the greatest care. The period furniture shimmered like satin from years of careful polishing, the colours were muted, peachy and a subtle sage green, and on the walls were oriental portraits against gold leaf backgrounds. The whole apartment had such a feeling of space and calm that if she'd told me she was a Zen Buddhist I wouldn't have been surprised.

In her bedroom my eyes almost flew out of my head, for on her dressing table were matched brush, comb, hand mirror and small cheval glass, all designed in delicate art nouveau silver in a style reproduced years later by every jobbing jeweller in London. She took me to a large theatrical skip, where she said I would find the basis of her wardrobe for the film. She was absolutely right; I think the one thing she wore in *Morgan* not provided by herself was a well-worn cotton overall which belonged to my Irish housekeeper. The only other actress I have known with the same wonderfully true instinct about the right clothes for a character part was Edith Evans who, when she was to play Ma Tanner in the film of *Look Back in Anger*, went shopping with me at Arding and Hobbs and Woolworths in Clapham, and borrowed her shoes, stockings and handbag from her own housekeeper.

Whilst working on *Morgan*, I was also designing Jeanne Moreau's clothes for *Mademoiselle*, with just enough time for a final fitting between her return from Mexico, where she was filming *Viva Maria* with Brigitte Bardot, and the start of shooting. Jeanne's clothes were to be made by Pierre Cardin, the only person she would trust to do that in her absence: there wasn't a concavity or convexity of her body he didn't know by heart. I left for Paris and a meeting with Pierre Cardin, taking merely hand luggage and the folder of my carefully finished drawings. These were bundled into the boot of the producer Oscar Lewenstein's car when he called for me, and off we set for London Airport, driven by his secretary. Somewhere en route the boot flew open, my suitcase and the drawings flew out, and by the time someone had attracted our attention it was too late. Distraught, I wanted to stay behind and search, but Oscar insisted I continue to Paris, where we ultimately arrived to find Tony waiting with Pierre Cardin.

Stopping only to brush my hair, I went to Tony's suite. He was soothing and sympathetic and put a strong drink into my shaking hands. Pierre Cardin kept saying, 'Écoute Josceleene, I was a theatrical designer myself; sit down and scribble them on the back of an envelope.' At this point, for which I shall always be grateful, Tony took over and said, 'Everyone leave her alone, she's upset. Let her go back to London for a week and re-draw the designs in her own studio.' Which is what I did. The last word went to Jan, Tony's driver, who said on the way to Orly Airport, 'If Oscar used a professional driver this would never have happened.' No drawings ever turned up, despite my London address and the address of my hotel in Paris being on the folder. The film company, Woodfall, offered a reward for them – but they never surfaced again. In my mind's eye I see them hanging as gloomy decorations on the wall of some semi on the Great West Road.

My re-drawn designs didn't have the same degree of finish as the first lot, but at least they contained the same information. Whenever I start designing I begin literally scribbling over the large sheets in a layout pad of semi-transparent paper. From these scribbles the final designs emerge, added to, or simplified until what I have arrived at has the right feeling for the particular scene to be played. Then, taking a sheet of watercolour paper, I transcribe my initial pencil scribbles into a finished ink and watercolour drawing, plus — and this is almost more important to me than the drawing — arrows pointing to various parts of the costume. I write, by these, meticulous notes about how I want it cut, how I wish a sleeve to be finished, a shoulder seam dropped, or a collar set at a certain distance from the neck. Although the task of re-drawing all Jeanne's costumes was a waste of valuable time from Cardin's point of view, for me it simply meant referring back to the original scribbles.

I returned to Paris, and Pierre Cardin and I went through them together. Next day he sent people all over the city for the right kind of fabrics, and I pinned the pieces of my choice to each drawing. At the end, he gently took my hands between his, pecked my cheeks and said, 'Now go back to London and don't worry. I'll telephone when the clothes are ready for you to look at.'

In the midst of all this hectic activity, just before Easter, John Osborne rang me to say he was directing a play by Charles Wood, *Meals on Wheels*, at the Royal Court; Alan Tagg was doing the sets, would I do the costumes, which he wanted based on Donald McGill's seaside postcards? First I said much as I wanted to I didn't see how I could. Then I thought about it, rang John back, and asked about the number of characters and costume changes. We finally decided that if I went down to Hellingly over Easter and I didn't do anything except draw, I would just be able to get the whole lot done between the Thursday night and Tuesday morning.

Ruth Myers who, for eleven pounds a week, was running the Royal Court wardrobe, turned out to be the most hardworking and inspired collaborator. She would work all day by herself, and at night we would work together. It was a real essay in economy. We bought white trousers and jackets from a shop in Soho that sold clothes for waiters and chefs, and dyed them brilliant primary colours; we hammered bottle tops flat and attached them to ribbons to make up rows of medals; and Ruth conjured up for one actress a confection of

My mother with my sister Pauline, 1908

Nanny and me aged eighteen months

My sisters Pauline and Sheila with their friend Ruth McNicoll (*right*)

With my father in 1942

Harry Tatlock Miller, me and Loudon
Sainthill at Fernhill, 1946

The Merioola Group: (*left to right*) Arthur Fleischmann, Alison Lee, Justin
O'Brien, Donald Friend, Loudon Sainthill, Harry Tatlock Miller, Edgar Ritchard,
me up ladder, Chica Edgeworth, Alec Murray and Roland Strasse.

With Rafael Kubelik and Deta de Ranitz
at my first show in Sidney, 1946

With Freddie Ayer

Alec Murray

John Hayward, Graham Greene, me and a friend at Battersea Funfair

Nelo Risi

Painting a backdrop for the
Diaghilev Exhibition

With John Osborne in Portmeirion

With Raoul Coutard on location for *The Sailor From Gibraltar*

Some of the costumes for *Blow-Up*

Shirley MacLaine in *The Bliss of Mrs Blossom*

My design for a bodyguard and (*right*) Michael York plus bodyguards in *Alfred the Great*

The design and finished costume for Sarah Miles's first scene in *Ryan's Daughter*

John Mills and Robert Mitchum in *Ryan's Daughter*

With my husband Clive on location in Shrewsbury

multi-coloured rollers and a huge hairnet which she could take on and off like a hat.

It was fascinating working at the same time on three such different productions, which ranged from the extreme refinement of Pierre Cardin's couture house, where I only had to express a wish to see it immediately carried out, to finding myself, at the end of an already tiring working day, kneeling on a dusty floor hammering away at Coca-Cola bottle tops. But this triple experience, though interesting, taught me that it's not advisable to work on more than one job at a time. It takes a very heavy toll, especially on someone who, like me, possesses a one-track mind.

The time came for me to return to Paris, meet Jeanne Moreau, and see how she and the clothes responded to each other. The day before we were due to meet, Pierre showed me the costumes on one of his house models, which gave the proceedings a slightly surrealist effect as she displayed them all as though she were showing the Cardin collection to a group of New York buyers. Nevertheless, the effect was extraordinary, and I was filled with delight; it was as though my drawings had come alive. Pierre gently warned me, however, about something of which I was all too aware. He said, 'Joseleene, I have respected your drawings totally, but it is possible that Jeanne will not like them – she's not used to wearing theese sort of clothes.'

The following evening, taking Nino Caprioglio with me – as a fashion artist his understanding of clothes would be a great support – I went to Cardin's first-floor room. The *mise-en-scène* was perfect: everything had been cleared away except the costumes. These were ranged in rows, with matching stockings, all the shawls and scarves neatly folded, shoes in perfect colour for every dress including high-heeled black patent leather ones and crocheted lace gloves to satisfy the eponymous Mademoiselle's particular eccentricities. Pierre, Nino and I waited, rather tense, saying nothing to each other. Punctually Jeanne arrived, having come home from Mexico the day before with a suntan and blonde hair. For her role in *Mademoiselle* we had to bleach her skin and dye her hair *chatain*. She was accompanied by two hatchet-faced women; all three of them wore little black dresses and mink coats. I hate an audience at fittings, and in London I would have removed them to another room. I glanced at Pierre; his reaction was clearly the same as mine and our eyes met in disapproval; but as he said nothing I clearly couldn't. I was introduced to Jeanne; we started the fitting. Pierre did everything himself, carrying in his breast pocket a tiny pair of very sharp scissors, the handpiece I think in the shape of a gold bird. With each change of costume there was a running commentary from the attendant acolytes. I was getting ready to seize Pierre's scissors and plunge them into their hearts, when Jeanne, suddenly sizing up the situation, said she would meet them later for dinner. After that the fitting went very professionally, and Jeanne's requests for changes were all to do with the comfort one needs while acting: technical demands and totally justified.

Eventually it was over. Jeanne left for dinner and Pierre and I went through lists and delivery dates together. By now I was prepared to cut off both hands for him; he had stage-managed me through the most difficult fitting of my life so far, and I felt nothing but an overwhelming admiration and affection for him. Nino and I went back to the St Raphael where I was staying, ordered dinner, went through all his notes and mine, and finally, in a state of euphoria, drank a bottle of champagne as a nightcap before he left and I dropped into bed.

I returned to London, tidied up loose ends on *Morgan*, packed up and set out for the shooting of *Mademoiselle* in Correze, a very beautiful part of France, full of rivers, rolling hills, woods, and trout streams. The average age of its people was nearing seventy, and de Gaulle had clearly felt that this gave him a brutal opportunity. They were very poor, would soon be dead, and he could then build a nuclear power station without opposition. I found this the most chilling political decision I had ever heard of, and it was no small wonder to me that the aged people of Correze were ardent communists.

Despite the beauty of the country, one of the bleakest villages in all France, appropriately named le Rat, was chosen for the main location. It had the necessary hard-edged quality of poverty suggested in the script. It was without any kind of softness and totally bereft of charm. The tiny village square was devoid of any vegetation, so we had to import our own fully-grown pollarded plane trees: and when, at the end of the shooting, they were found to have actually taken root and bravely put out shoots, the village elders refused to accept them even as a present – they preferred their square unsoftened by nature.

The square was bounded on three sides by buildings, parts of which we were able to use for production offices, the wardrobe, workroom, stock room, and dressing-rooms. In the rest of the village we found interiors and exteriors which, with a very little set dressing, we used for some of the main sets.

We had a good French crew, and French crews are anyway more open-minded and less departmentalized than English or American ones. A film crew comprises everyone from the director to a runner. They all work together for the good of the film, rather than as individuals. It doesn't occur to a French wardrobe mistress to refuse to make a pair of cotton curtains because officially it's someone else's job, and nobody would threaten a strike if I were to help the camera crew by carrying a piece of their equipment.

Of course, for a movie to be well serviced by its technicians is not enough. *Mademoiselle*, lovingly photographed by David Watkin, should have emerged as a marvellous study of a rural community. Instead, Jeanne was favoured so much in the editing that the film became a portrait of a psychopath with insufficient motivation, and was vaguely unsatisfactory and melodramatic.

Once it was finished, Tony immediately went into pre-production with the same technical crew on *The Sailor from Gibraltar*, except that the great French cinematographer Raoul Coutard took over from David Watkin. Again Jeanne Moreau starred with a cast that included Vanessa Redgrave, Umberto Orsini, Orson Welles and Ian Bannen. It was to start shooting in Florence, go to Agropoli and Paestum in the south of Italy, then on to Athens, Egypt and I don't remember where else because in Athens Tony and I, it seems, parted company forever. From the very beginning, the film had lacked organization. Tony and I had started out with the idea that as the character played by Jeanne constantly sailed the world in her yacht, her clothes should reflect the ethnic look of her last port of call. Tony changed his mind, however, and asked me to go to Cardin with Jeanne. There she chose some unsuitable clothes that I knew wouldn't photograph well, but she was in no mood to be argued with and that seemed to be that.

As time went on, and we travelled from place to place with the speed of light, the work became increasingly tough going for me and for Ruth Myers, my assistant. Among other problems, we were dressing a big cast production with a scandalously understaffed wardrobe. This all came to a head when, in Athens, I started to show Tony a supply of new clothes. Astonishingly, he greeted me with,

'You know you're going back to England today to work on *The Charge of the Light Brigade*?' This, despite my work on *The Sailor From Gibraltar* being nowhere near finished. I have rarely been angrier in my life. I had time only to show him the clothes, which I think were for Ian Bannen, to talk to Ruth, whose first experience of filming this was, and to say goodbye to the French technicians, with whom by now I had a marvellous working relationship. Everyone, as I kissed them goodbye, said '*Tu blagues! Pourquoi?*' Tony's associate producer, Neil Hartley, drove me to the hotel to pack and then to the airport, where I wrote Tony a note telling him he knew what he could do with *The Charge of the Light Brigade*. I had no intention of working with him again. Later I asked, whether successfully or not I don't know, for my name to be taken off the credits for *The Sailor From Gibraltar*, as I hadn't had time to do half the work I had been engaged for, and what would be seen on the screen wouldn't be my choice. It was a very dismal state of affairs, and no one has ever been able to explain satisfactorily to me why Tony behaved as he did.

After years of reflection I think the real reason was that my friendship with Simone Knapp (Jeanne's *maquilleuse*) and Raoul Coutard caused Jeanne considerable jealousy, and she probably put pressure on Tony to send me back to London. She, as I knew her then, was an odd mixture of charm and capriciousness. One day she would be gay, and cook one a delicious dinner of black Perigord truffles in champagne and brandy served with plain boiled potatoes, and the next her eyes would turn beady and suspicious as she watched one's every move from the sidelines. She had for years, apparently, ever since *Jules et Jim*, tried to annexe Coutard for herself. When she suddenly noticed that he and I frequently dined together or simply sat talking on the set between takes, her reaction was sufficient to make Simone come to me and say, '*Chérie, garde-toi* – Jeanne is asking questions about you and Raoul.' My relationship with her during *Mademoiselle* was ideal, but during *The Sailor From Gibraltar* it withered away to the point that I didn't even bother to say goodbye to her.

Weeks later, when the shooting was finished, Vanessa suddenly rang me in a highly emotional state. Could she come to see me? She arrived on the doorstep with tears streaming down her face. She said she had come straight from John and Penelope whom she'd been questioning about her marriage to Tony and whether they thought it was collapsing. They had laughed at her, so she had come to ask me. I said I wished she hadn't, but she proceeded to quizz me like a QC. Because she seemed to think the remainder of her life was at stake, I answered her questions truthfully, but with the proviso that when she confronted Tony with what I had told her she would promise to tell him she had come to me seeking specific information. Whether she ever did that, I don't know. But to Tony my conversation with Vanessa was a betrayal; and every time a version of what I said comes back to me, it takes on different and more elaborate forms, none bearing any relation to the reality. It was in fact a tempest in a teacup. I only hope they're both now settled down happily, he with the demon bitch of his choice – Hollywood – and Vanessa, God help her, with the Workers Revolutionary Party; though without these respective partners, Vanessa would, I believe, be an even more superlative actress and Tony would have more fully realized his promise as the one really creative young film producer working in England at that time.

I just wish Vanessa hadn't confided in me about youthful affairs and marital problems caused by her and Tony's lack of real concern for each other, and their inability to cope with each other's complexities. By off-loading the mess that was her emotional life into my lap, all she succeeded in doing was cutting me off forever from two friends – herself and Tony – and of the two, Tony was the one I valued most and most miss.

The whole miserable business had truly old-fashioned repercussions from time to time, with Tony declaring, 'I'll never work with that woman in films again.' Later, Oscar Lewenstein, talking to Evangeline Harrisson, announced quite simply that I was 'the wickedest woman in the world', a view he shared with Renée Ayer and Stuart Hampshire. I can't think of three more desirable enemies.

Back in London and relieved to be away from it all, tired out and suffering from influenza, I put my feet up and read thrillers until I felt human again. And eighteen months later there was one pleasingly ironic postscript to this part of my life. My agent, Pat Chard of London Management, asked me to be sure to attend the BAFTA Awards Ceremony at Grosvenor House because they were absolutely certain I was going to win one. Apparently there were only two nominations for best costume design for a black-and-white movie, and both were for me: for *Mademoiselle* and, funnily enough, for *The Sailor From Gibraltar*. In those days the award was a fragile black basalt figure mounted on a wooden base and called 'Stella'. After collecting mine which, as it turned out, was for *Mademoiselle*, I sat with friends and watched fascinated as Edith Evans and Paul Scofield, while receiving theirs, lent forward to kiss each other. For the necks of their 'Stellas' engaged, and both award-winners were left with decapitated trophies in their hands, 'Stellas'' heads rolling round their feet.

XIII

In 1965 it was announced that Michelangelo Antonioni was coming to London to make a film. I longed to work with him, but at that time I had no agent to approach him on my behalf, and couldn't think of any way of approaching him myself. The more I read about the forthcoming film, the more obsessed I became with it. Then one morning Assheton Gorton telephoned me to say he was working with Antonioni, and he, Assheton, wanted me to work with him, but his real reason for ringing was that he would like to show Antonioni my studio at 7 Pembroke Studios, and any other studios I could get the keys to, as possible locations.

I said, 'Yes, bring him round, but you mustn't put him in a tight corner about engaging me; for all he knows I might be the worst designer in the world; please don't, in front of me, let him think I'm anything other than a painter.'

Just about lunchtime they arrived: Assheton, Antonioni and Tonnino Guerro, his scriptwriter. I showed them Leonard's studio, mine, and several others. But all of them were too small for what was in his mind. We shook hands and said goodbye.

Three quarters of an hour later Assheton telephoned again to say that he hadn't promised not to say I was a designer once he got back into the car, and that Antonioni had looked at him and said, 'You don't think she is too sophisticated for me?' to which Assheton had replied, 'She's a simple girl at heart.'

The upshot was that I was asked to present myself at Antonioni's St James's Street offices as soon as I could. Within half an hour I was there, a treatment of the film was put into my hand – it was at this stage simply called 'The Antonioni Film'; it had yet to become *Blow-Up* – and I was given an empty office to read it in. After I'd done that, and I had never read anything so full of visual possibilities, I was taken to Antonioni, who said in Italian, 'Do you speak Italian?' I replied, 'Only kitchen Italian.' He frowned and muttered to himself about the impossibility of communication. But I wanted to hang on so I said, 'Francese?' His face cleared and from that moment, and for nearly a year, we spoke French together. He and Assheton communicated by osmosis, as neither spoke any language known to the other.

Without any doubt *Blow-Up* is the film I have most enjoyed working on. The conception of the film was almost entirely visual, because not only did Antonioni think in clearly defined visual terms but also the subject of the film concerned a successful young fashion photographer who, while prowling through an alien part of London, takes a series of photographs of a grassy stretch of parkland with a dense outcrop of trees in the middle distance. When he develops the film and starts printing, he crops the negative and blows up the trees, bigger and still bigger, until in grainy blow-ups of the dense thicket of vegetation, he realizes that he has actually photographed the story of a murder. The film fulfilled and stretched me more than any other – in part because it was such knife-edge work. Antonioni could really only judge a costume through the camera, in the right setting, and consequently I had to get it right first time. There was also, it must be said, the new and wonderful feeling of working for an organization, MGM, who paid well, after the somewhat parsimonious Woodfall.

Antonioni's approach to the design of the film was to look two years into the future of fashion. So I went to Paris and researched the fashion houses and fabric manufacturers. I saw many wonders, including a molten silver tissue that moved like water flowing from a tap, and a matt white jersey that changed colour under different lights.

One of the main locations for the film were a large warehouse which had been converted into a photographic studio and house, and this Assheton transformed into something infinitely more interesting. From the living-room floor he built two gantries, which ran the whole length of the studio to the dark-rooms with their stark white doors, through which one could glimpse the red working lights as David Hemmings frantically assembled the entire series of blown-up prints. Another main location was an eighteenth-century house on the river in Cheyne Walk which was filled for two nights with the *jeunnesse dorée* of London, who were allowed to wear only black, white or silver. Once they were all dressed I went in to cast my eye over the exotic collection of young London beauties. The air was heavy with the smell of marijuana, so strong it made me feel dizzy and sick.

Another important location was a park in south-east London. Assheton had got permission to have the road through it painted black, the houses that overlooked it clad with white-painted fronts, and the grass sprayed a brilliant clear green because the summer sun had scorched it yellow. It was here, at the end of the film, that the mysterious tennis match took place, played without rackets and without balls, the sound track recorded with Antonioni himself playing. In his youth he had been a tennis champion.

I found him endlessly fascinating and attractive. He was slight and dark, his face like an El Greco, with dark hair and even darker eyes. He was a highly intellectually cultivated man, which is what made his question about my being possibly 'too sophisticated' nothing short of hilarious. He possessed great sensibility and a reserved, slightly withdrawn manner, and was always punctiliously polite unless we were having a row, when he would withdraw completely – but so did I, and once a week passed without our addressing a single word to the other, until one morning he looked at me, roared with laughter, and said, '*Assieds-toi, Jocelyn. Qu'est-ce que tu as?*' Rarely for a film director, he started life as a painter, but believing he might never be good enough, he turned his gift for composition to movie-making. When he abandoned black and white films for colour his use of colour was exactly like a painter's. This was, I think, one of the reasons we were able to work together so well. I only ever produced one colour he didn't like: '*Vert d'olive – oh, Jocelyn, c'est tellement triste.*'

After we'd been shooting for some months, Antonioni decided to edit as much film as he'd shot, so as to make sure how much more he needed. At this point, all I could think of was taking off for somewhere warm, and lying down. I had been told about the Centre Culturel in Hammamet, which sounded ideal and in the event proved perfect. Run by the Tunisian Government, it was totally geared to pampering tired 'intellectuals' and artists, though one had first to be introduced and then invited to stay.

We – that is, Leonard and I (we just managed to get along if we weren't left alone together too much) – arrived after dark and were taken to a small villa set in the garden of a large house, the villa typically Arab with a domed roof, its own terrace, and scented by orange and lemon blossom and the even headier perfume of a double datura which grew against the walls.

Waking in the morning in a strange and beautiful place is, for me, one of the greatest delights of life. At first light, I prowled in the garden, which was planted with only white flowers and bisected by narrow winding paths: a square mile bordered on one side by the Mediterranean and opposite by a high wall hiding the road. The main house, built in the twenties by an aristocratic German homosexual, was very simple and quite marvellously stylish. The ceilings were high and vaulted, the doors wooden and heavy and decorated with nail heads. I have said elsewhere in this book that I've never seen an aesthetically pleasing swimming-pool. I'd forgotten Hammamet, where the vast marble pool was surrounded by a perfect white marble colonnade, and filled with clear sparkling water which was the same pale green as lemonade bottles. A huge table at one end, made out of a single immense block of granite that looked like basalt or polished slate, was one of the most beautiful pieces of furniture I have ever seen.

On top of the house was an exquisite seraglio apartment with pierced screens surrounding it, and views stretching into infinity in every direction. During the desert campaign the house was Rommel's headquarters, and the seraglio his personal apartment.

The food, served under a vine-covered trellis close to the kitchens and away from the house, was a subtle mixture of Arab and French cuisine, deliciously full of delicate spices. The Tunisian wine, red and chilled, was light and didn't rush straight to the head; Bokkah, a lethal spirit made from figs and often drunk with Coca-Cola was available to the foolish; and the mineral water, which I found myself calling 'heavy water', raced through one's system with the same speed as Turkish tripe soup.

As always in a new place, I cautiously asked for a table for two, wishing to observe first and make friends later. But on the evening of the second day, just as dinner was about to be served, there appeared a familiar figure dressed in a white djellabah, face sunburned, eyes gleaming like star sapphires – the choreographer John Cranko. I hadn't seen him during the time I'd lived with John Osborne and he'd been in Germany putting the Stuttgart Ballet on the map. We wrapped our arms round each other, both talking at once, John, amazed, pointing at Leonard and shouting, 'You're not married to each other?'

There is nothing John and I didn't know about each other. We could be silent together, or gossip like fishwives. We could talk about his family, or laugh about his lovers. We were ideal friends, a heterosexual and a homosexual who loved each other and were totally uncritical; who always accepted the whole of each other. That night – and every night for the rest of our stay – we dined together, and as we lingered over our last glasses of wine, he and I, as we had often done before, started singing old songs very softly. John was the only person who ever said anything nice about my singing voice. 'You sing,' he would say, 'a perfect second...'

Between the end of the garden and the beach, in a natural declivity, a miniature Greek amphitheatre had been built; the acoustics, certainly on a still night, were pin sharp. Theatre companies like Roger Planchon's, or John Cranko's ballet group, would play there for a short season. But during the time of Leonard's and my stay there were no performances, and sometimes after dinner we would all take cushions and lie there, gossiping in the moonlight. One night, out of the dark, Robert Namia, a left-wing French writer with whom we'd become friendly, turned his head and asked, 'You know John Leetle-hoode?' I thought wildly of Robin Hood and Maid Marian, and eventually said no. He persisted: 'John Leetlehoode, the celebrated English deerector.' My mind was still blank until he added, '*Mais cette dame est bien connue,*' and I realized whom he was talking about. Joan Littlewood and her lover and partner Gerry Raffles had, said Robert, brought a production to Hammamet the previous year, accompanied by her aged father, who had never seen the sea before and was perfectly content to spend the whole two weeks looking at the Mediterranean, propped up with cushions in a boat carefully beached and wedged in the sand, an umbrella over his head to shade him from the sun and a supply of goodies to eat and drink.

John Cranko would use our bathroom at breakfast time. Once there was a yell and I went in to find him as ashen-faced as his suntan would allow. 'You don't think I've got the clap do you?' he said, displaying several incipient boils on his behind. 'Not there you haven't,' I replied, seizing a bottle of Dettol and some cotton wool swabs. I dressed his tail with care and said I'd take him to the

National Health Clinic in Hammamet; Leonard decided to come too – he had earache. There, quantities of sand and seaweed were syringed out of Leonard's ear, and he was given a shot of antibiotic. John, having removed his trousers and underpants and bent over, his head hanging between his legs, suddenly saw the black face of the Arab doctor on a level with his own saying, '*Oh, M. Cranko, je suis ravi de faire votre connaissance.*' John too was given antibiotics, but he didn't have the clap; he was just overworked and run down.

During this perfect holiday I was too tired to do any serious sightseeing, apart from going to the Bardo, the great Tunisian Museum where the remains of ancient Carthage hang like giant jewels on the walls. Carthage itself, in 1965, I found hard to come to terms with: just masses of flattened rubble, a place to be passed while going to Sidi Bou Said. This is one of the most perfect of all small Arab towns, rich and immaculate, all the houses looking as though they'd been painted the week before. Its streets rise and dip, and small flights of steps lead to miraculous vistas of the sea glimpsed through the architecture. Best of all, on the way there one crosses a small estuary and each moving car puts up a flight of cloud after rose pink cloud of flamingos.

We lunched on the outskirts of Sidi Bou Said with Cecil Hourani, the then Minister of Culture, who lived in the one house I have wanted more than any other in the world: a fourteenth-century palace built round a central courtyard filled with jasmine. Corridors of patterned tiles led into vast salons, one opening out of the other, these exquisitely tiled also. Nowhere else have I seen a design so sumptuous yet so subtle.

Luncheon, served in a comparatively small room – for about twenty people – was as superb as the house. A refectory table was covered with a straw-coloured organza cloth embroidered in gold silk; delicate Limoges porcelain was laid on top of silver gilt plate; the knives, forks and spoons were gold; wine was served in antique glass, and water in elaborate silver gilt goblets. Despite all this splendour, the food was still good enough to remember. We began the meal with fragile triangular pastries filled with tabbouleh and raw egg, which were deep fried until the egg was lightly cooked but still runny; Tunisian etiquette required these delicious morsels be eaten with the fingers without the egg yolk dribbling down your arm. The couscous which followed was a perfect blend of chicken and lamb cooked with saffron, cinnamon and honey, and served with a selection of crisp young vegetables.

All too quickly the six weeks in Hammamet passed. As they came to an end, I could hear in my head the siren call of Antonioni about to finish his film. John and Robert Namia came to the airport with us, and this was alas the last time I ever saw John. Tragically he had a heart attack and died in a plane *en route* from New York to Stuttgart.

Back in London, Antonioni was indeed ready to start shooting again. But the night-club he'd chosen earlier as a special location was by now pulled down, so it had to be painstakingly recreated in MGM's studios. Of more concern to me personally was the discovery that the dark green corduroy jacket which David Hemmings had worn throughout the film had been stolen by some light-fingered passer-by. To anyone not used to working on movies such a loss would seem merely an irritation. But with four months of film shot in which the star was dressed in this particular jacket, it was a disaster; and we had only until eight o'clock the following morning to come up with another exactly the same. I rang Bermans and told the man who'd been with me when I first found the jacket, at the Shaftesbury Avenue Cecil Gee, that I'd send him a car and would he please scour London. For four hours Rebecca Breed, the wardrobe mistress, and I waited in a state of despairing inertia. Then our misery was relieved, at least partly. The colour of the jacket we were given when the car got back was a perfect match; the pocket details were all different, however. Rebecca didn't think we'd get away with it. But a little subtle stitching of pockets so that they didn't gape made it fairly unlikely that anyone would notice. They didn't. Of such miniscule details are the crises of film-making made up.

I went to America in mid-December for the opening of *Blow-Up*. Leonard, who had won a Churchill Fellowship and was going to travel round the States for six months, came with me. I'm conscious that I've so far said very little about Leonard. Now is perhaps the time to fill in the details.

He is eleven years older than I, but looks eternally youthful. He had a painful childhood, was used as a weapon between warring parents, and grew up hating his father, so much so, in fact, that he even refused to learn to drive, because of particularly bad memories of his father's raffish driving. His passion in life is his work.

I first began to notice his painting, in English magazines, while I was still living in Australia, and oddly enough, he came to Australia as an official war artist attached to the Marines, and lived next door to Merioola far a few weeks of leave. Once the war was over he went to Edinburgh College of Art and taught mural painting and, at the same time, maintained a small apartment in London above Olwen Vaughan's French Club. It was at this time that I first met him, and as a friend he was charming and engaging, if a little chilly.

He left Edinburgh when he was offered the same sort of job at the Royal College of Art. Unlike Freddie, who gave his all to his pupils, Leonard kept a great deal of himself in reserve, as though frightened he might otherwise give his talent away. My concern was that he would dissipate his talent by spreading it thinly over too wide a field – illustrations, book jackets, murals and easel paintings. It is as an easel painter that he is at his best, though sometimes guilty of either under- or overworking a painting. But this usually evens out in the end, as he is capable of reworking a painting over a number of years. I may not love the man, but I certainly admire his work.

Whilst in New York for *Blow-Up* I decided, because I had never been there before, that I wanted to stay on for a while after the première and have a look about. MGM had opened *Grand Prix*, a film on which they had spent millions, and *Blow-Up*, a film on which they had spent only thousands, in the same week. They had expected that *Grand Prix* would take off like a rocket; *Blow-Up* they had thought of as what they called an 'Art House Movie' which might just recover its costs, but would do them good because they would get prestige from it. They were totally unprepared for *Grand Prix* to sink without trace, and *Blow-Up* to soar to success.

But by then, apart from me, there was no one in New York who could help MGM even caption a photograph, let alone help to meet the demands for publicity. Antonioni had returned to Italy; Vanessa Redgrave and David Hemmings were in Hollywood, both contractually obliged to go on filming *Camelot* – Vanessa playing Guinevere and David playing Mordred in what has to be one of the worst films ever made.

In Europe at this time girls were wearing skirts like wide belts slung low on their hips, and I walked into the MGM offices on Sixth Avenue in a tweed miniskirt, thick tights, polo-necked pullover, flat-heeled high suede boots, and a leather cap. The three receptionists sitting behind their desks with skirts to mid-calf, and faces as pretty as

flowers, all drew in their breath and let it out again in a long
mellifluous hiss. In one voice they said, 'They won't let us wear
skirts that length in here.' We exchanged thoughts on that. Then I
said I'd come to see someone called Milt in charge of publicity.
Milt and two cronies were puffing away at cigars the size of table
legs, lolling back in large leather armchairs, with a rosy post-pran-
dial glaze to their features. 'You must meet Lily,' said Milt. Lily
was small dark and Jewish and very, very funny. I was handed over
to her, as to a nanny. Lily was to organize whatever space they
could hope to get for me in the press, on television, or on radio; in
return they would pick up my bill at the Algonquin.

These were the days long before the women's liberation move-
ment was even into first gear, and from what followed in the media
it appeared that I alone in New York knew where I was going and
was stripped for action, whereas New York women were the
dowdiest collection of drabs I'd ever set eyes on. One typical
headline proclaimed: 'No one in Europe wears lingerie any more,'
and the interview below it made it seem that I thought every good
Little Rock lady should flush her undies down what Americans
refer to as 'the John'. No doubt this story grew from my mild statement that the models in *Blow-Up* didn't wear knickers or bras
because I didn't want unsightly bumps under their clothes.

However, it was all good publicity for the film and I talked
myself hoarse to such a degree that MGM suggested I might like to
continue talking my way across the States from New Orleans to
Los Angeles. I thanked them but said no and goodbye. That
treat, if so it is, was something the future held in store for me.

During the time I was in New York I saw a great deal of Marian
Cummings, the widow of e. e. cummings, who as Marian
Moorehouse had been the first great name model. I had known
them both a long time. Her beauty was serene and indestructible,
but from the moment she fell in love with cummings she seemed to
shroud her superb looks in protective colouring, so that she could
pass unnoticed through the world. In New York she still lived in
the house in Patchin Place that she and cummings had shared for
many years. There she, the least hysterical of women, brought
home to me the horror, even then, of a woman living alone in New
York. Inside the front door she kept a fully loaded shot-gun, and
whenever she went out she carried a Japanese paper knife, housed

in a bamboo sheath, but filed to the sharpness of a lethal ice pick or stiletto.

Marian was the only person in New York I was really sorry to say goodbye to. There are times when one's goodbye proves to be the last and, as with John Cranko, so it was with Marian. I was in New York again fairly soon but she, by then, was dead of cancer.

When I arrived back in London, I had to kick my way through a pile of accumulated mail, which included a fat package of yellowing press cuttings, lodged behind the front door. It appeared that some London journalists had sent me up rotten about the interviews I'd given in the New York papers. To a few of them I wrote a feeble protest, but it wasn't even yesterday's news, it was last month's, and no one was anxious to spoil a funny story. Leonard was an ardent devotee of Durrants Press Cutting Services, otherwise I would never have known what had been said about me, and to be honest I didn't really care. I was just enjoying being once more in a city where one felt safe. At night I would stop taxis about a mile from Pembroke Studios so that I could enjoy walking the rest of the way home.

Very soon after I'd got back I worked on a Kevin Billington film, *Interlude*, which on the whole went as smoothly as silk. I like young, untried directors as Kevin was then; their enthusiasm and energy is infectious. The only drawback is that their lack of experience is apt to make them hold you to them with the grip of a boa-constrictor. But I was anyway forced to slither out of Kevin's grasp because I was also starting to design the costumes for another film, *The Bliss of Mrs Blossom*, directed by Joe McGrath, with Shirley MacLaine, Richard Attenborough and James Booth. For this I needed a good assistant, and Assheton Gorton, who was designing the sets, produced Evangeline Harrison – whom I had met once before when we were shooting *Morgan*. Ten years younger than I, she proved the perfect choice. Trained at Central Art School, Glyndebourne and Stratford, she had taken time off to produce two children and was aching to start work again. I liked everything about her. We had the same sort of taste and spoke the same kind of language, and she could stand up to me, which I like. We settled into a long and happy collaboration which has become a close and abiding friendship. She and Alec are still the only people I welcome if they ring the doorbell without announcing beforehand that they are coming.

Whilst these films were moving ahead, I had a telephone call from

Robert Namia saying he was coming to London. We arranged to meet, with his daughter, who was learning English as an *au pair*. The evening of his arrival he was as intelligent and witty as he'd appeared to be in the hot summer sun of Hammamet, and just as attractive. What I'd thought of then as a probability became a fact: we became lovers, and it was this which saved me during the wearisome tensions of what was to be the last year or so of my inglorious marriage to Leonard. Namia gave me a key to his apartment in Paris and the freedom to use it whenever I felt I had to get away. It was a safety valve that saw me through endless bitter arguments.

At my insistence, Leonard had made friends with Ginette again. I couldn't see how a thirteen years' love could be so easily put aside. My feelings for her and hers towards me never changed. I had never liked her and never could. But she and Leonard once more became very close right up until the time Leonard and I divorced, and I believe she would have married him after her husband, Robin Darwin, later died, had Leonard by then not been otherwise engaged.

XIV

It was Easter in 1967 and once again I went down to Hellingly to work. By now John Osborne and Penelope, all too inevitably, had parted. Penelope had always viewed the prospect of pregnancy with horror; she believed she would feel as though she were carrying in her belly a rat which would gnaw at her identity. Once she discovered she was pregnant with Nolan, her attitude changed. When the child was born, Penelope took refuge in work to distance herself from John and then was surprised to find that he was getting on without her with the help of Jill Bennett, whom she had deputed to 'look after Johnny'.

That Easter Jill was in Turkey filming *The Charge of the Light Brigade*, with Tony Richardson directing. I had known her for almost all the time I'd lived in London; she was a close friend of Leonard's and together they would play childlike games of who could tell the biggest whoppers. Eventually Jill and John married, after which he and I became separated – that is until they, too, parted. But that is now so far in the past I scarcely remember there was a time when John and I for a while didn't communicate.

One of the happiest days of my life, and I'm certain of his too, was when John married the writer Helen Dawson. They live a life of palpable contentment in the country, without the resident entourage that both Jill and Penelope felt their status demanded. For the first time I witnessed a growing knowledge and love between John and a woman who is his equal, but who is not in the least professionally competitive.

But that Easter Sunday, as the designs for Shirley MacLaine were coming from the tip of my pen with happy ease, the telephone rang. It was the production manager of *The Bliss of Mrs Blossom*: Shirley MacLaine was on the jury of the Cannes Film Festival, so would I go to Cannes to meet her and Joe McGrath?

Cannes at Festival time is one of those places I would pay much to stay away from. I tried not to go, but for each argument I put forward another more pressing one came back. I finished up, as in the end I was bound to, hauling drawings and a suitcase full of marvellous fabrics I'd bought in the Marché St Pierre in Paris to Cannes, arriving on the Monday morning.

Yes, a room was reserved for me at the Carlton and one looking over the sea at that, so I couldn't feel too hardly done by; the sun was shining, and bar the shouting, the hideously crowded Festival was over. And, to my delight, *Blow-Up* had won the Palme d'Or.

In the late afternoon, Shirley MacLaine arrived wearing a pale blue dress, which made her eyes look as though they were cut from the same fabric. She was intelligent, charming and funny. She liked the drawings and liked the fabrics, so the journey had been worthwhile. I stayed on over the Tuesday, so that Joe, Shirley and I could go through the script together, and arranged to fly back to London on Wednesday morning. On Tuesday evening in the fading light as the Carlton terrace was becoming deserted and I was lingering over a last glass of champagne with the man from Paramount, I saw Nelo coming towards me with a tall Nordic woman whom I knew to be his second wife. He and I flew into each other's arms, and arranged to breakfast together next morning. Looking from my bedroom window I saw him arrive and went down to the terrace where we sat and talked. After some time I said, 'Do you notice anything strange about this conversation?'

'No, why?'

'We've talked for over three hours non-stop in French. When I was living with you I was so inarticulate and nervous I could never say anything that I really meant, I was too frightened of making a mistake, and when I left I vowed I would never allow myself to be in that position again. Because of you I learned to speak French.'

All too soon the car arrived to take me to the airport. As I left I reflected that the journey I hadn't wanted to make had provided me with a great bonus.

Assheton's set was growing at Twickenham Studios into a wonderful fairytale extravaganza. The premise of the film was simple. Mr

Blossom manufactured underclothes and had a secret passion for music, which he indulged by spending the evenings, as his wife painted, conducting to gramophone records. Mrs Blossom was a reclusive fantasist – the real world held no charm for her. Once home and cushioned in the 'do-it-yourself' art nouveau opulence of her own house she relaxed by cooking, painting, and sewing. But her sewing machine developed a fault and the Blossom factory engineer sent to repair it caught her fancy. She installed him in the attic. There he became for her the kind of lover who could fulfil her fantasies, which were triggered off by anything – a visual image, a phrase of music . . .

In all, Shirley as Mrs Blossom must have had about twenty-eight changes of costume. Amongst others, she imagined herself as Anna Karenina, Juliet, Madame Pompadour, a Venetian *commedia dell'arte* figure, an early filmstar, the maiden St George rescued from the dragon, the heroine of *Viva Zapata!* and Vigée le Brun.

I grew very fond of Shirley and she never failed to amuse me. But what no one had warned me of was that she hated being fitted. I only tried once. With a retinue from Bermans, the costumiers, I travelled to the house she had taken in Chertsey, where there developed such an unbelievable air of high lunacy that I packed the Bermans entourage off home and telephoned Joe for support, saying that if necessary I would wait at Chertsey all night for him. When he arrived and we were explaining to Shirley what we wanted I noticed that as soon as the word 'costume' was mentioned her eyes glazed over with boredom. I knew how she felt and frequently feel it myself. But I equally know that when working one somehow surmounts it. In this case we sent to Edith Head in Hollywood for Shirley's form, a three-dimensional figure made exactly to her measurements, and all her clothes were made on that. The night before shooting on a costume, we would have a fitting with Shirley and Brigit, the wardrobe mistress, who thankfully was handy with her needle, would let it out, take it in or leave it as it was. Next day, Shirley would blithely wear it as though she'd never caused us so much as a headache.

At the end of the filming, she packed all those fancy dresses and took them home with her. I often wonder why. Even in Hollywood they would look way, way over the top, unless she were planning to install Romeo, Count Vronsky, Louis XIV *et al.* in her attic and lead a rich fantasy life.

To Shirley the state of my marriage and my affair with 'the Frenchman', as she called Robert Namia, were a source of endless fascination. Even three years later when she glimpsed me across a crowded BAFTA Awards dinner, where she was seated, a model of witty dignity beside Lord Mountbatten, she cupped her mouth in her hands and silently megaphoned, 'Did you get rid of him?' I nodded yes, and then, hands to her mouth again, 'Well, what about the Frenchman?' 'Him too,' I semaphored back. 'You look much better for it,' she signed off.

The schedule for the film was long and beset with technical difficulties. One concerned Mr Blossom's invention of a spectacular bra, which at the touch of a button would inflate to a comely size. This was to be demonstrated in a sort of Miss World contest sequence. A crowd of nearly two thousand girls, some in polo-necked sleeveless leotards painted with their national flag, and each wearing their national headgear – either a bowler hat, or a Dutch bonnet, a spiked German helmet, or the Vatican mitre – were all, as their breasts inflated hugely, to rise like balloons to the roof, an essay in deliberate bad taste.

I had calculated that we needed three leotards for every girl – small, medium and large – to allow for maximum stretch. But before ordering such a large quantity of expensive American danceskins, I asked the American special effects man, Dick McDonald, if he would come to my studio and experiment. With his and his assistant's help I swam into a cumbersome nursing mother's bra, and wriggled into the smallest leotard. In seconds my natural thirty-four had enlarged to sixty inches with the amount of helium Dick McDonald had pumped into the bra, and I was rolling round the studio like a ball. But the idea worked, and without distorting the design painted on the leotard. In the event, the Miss Worlds drifted roofwards in one marvellous clean flight on their Kirby flying wires.

That caused another problem. Flying harnesses of leather and canvas which go between the legs and lace at the back like a corset are not meant to be worn all day, as was likely here; after half an hour they chafe. Vangie, Brigit and I looked thoughtfully at the Miss Worlds, and the Miss Worlds looked accusingly at us. 'Kotex,' I said, and before I knew what was happening they bundled me into a unit car with a pile of pound notes. It was eight-thirty in the morning, the nearest and largest Boots was just opening. I walked in and said to the kindest face I could find, 'I would like twelve dozen boxes of Kotex please.' She didn't bat an eyelid, but went over and whispered in the manager's ear, their eyes raking me from head to foot. 'Don't bother to wrap them, I'm in a hurry,' I said. It was only when the money had changed hands that I satisfied their curiosity. They looked more relieved than interested.

CHAPTER

XV

As *The Bliss of Mrs Blossom* drew to an end, Leonard was due back from the States and I felt I needed a bolt hole. With tremendous good luck I found one, in the middle of a block of three late Victorian studios in Roland Gardens. It was, once I'd put in a bathroom and kitchen, had the floor stripped to natural wood and the walls and ceilings painted white, exactly what I wanted.

It had belonged to Walter Sickert, who had installed a chimney piece that rivalled the Albert Memorial for extravagance of design. He felt so secure in its ambience that on seeing it in position he had exclaimed, 'Now I will paint my masterpiece.'

Cleaning it revealed an elaborately carved oak chimney breast reaching from the height of my head to the ceiling and standing on two dark green granite columns, each circled with a metal band on which were brass lions' heads with steel rings in their mouths. It had a very agreeable presence, and breathed out warmth as well as benignity. I felt I too, under its influence, might produce a masterpiece.

Leonard returned from the States not looking well. Before I left New York, Marian Cummings and I had both urged him to stop drinking because even two whiskies had a curious effect on him. However, now he was back I – selfishly – was more interested in my own concerns. I told him about Roland Gardens and Namia, about which I didn't expect him to be pleased. Nor was he. He was vituperative, and I deserved it. What no one deserved was the way the whisky which he drank to drown his sorrows seemed to poison him, and after God knows how many different tests it was discovered he was suffering from a rare virus that fed on and was aggravated by

111

alcohol. I don't know whether he still believes it was all caused by what he called my 'treacherous behaviour', but certainly at the time he did. His sympathetic doctor knew I wanted to leave him, but I agreed I should stay put until he recovered. We lived together in a state of grim truce until I was asked to design another location film, *M. le Coq*, with Zero Mostel, an actor whom everyone admired, but I secretly thought an only sometimes funny ham. Shooting on this did not however last long. One evening its director, Seth Holt, and I were working alone in his house and I heard what I thought was a tiny kitten mewing. Seth took no notice, so at the end of half an hour I said, 'Seth, you've locked a kitten in a cupboard.' He shook his head, 'No, my darling, I haven't. It's my asthmatic breathing.' So gentle and tactful was he that I didn't even feel I'd put my foot in it. But it was because of Seth's poor health, and a series of other reasons, like rising costs plus initial underbudgeting, that the film was shelved.

I was, as a consequence, still waiting for a location film that would give me a break from always being with Leonard when Alec telephoned in the middle of a week to ask if I was doing anything the following Saturday. Ever cautious I asked why. 'Well, if you're not, I thought you might like to come to my wedding,' he said. I was overjoyed. He had been having an affair for several years with a beautiful blonde Cornish model called Sue Robins, to whom I was devoted. She and Alec clearly loved each other but I'd despaired of their ever doing anything about it.

That Saturday, Leonard and I arrived at Eaton Square, on our way to Chelsea Registry Office, to find them both composed and excited, Sue looking ravishing in pink and natural coloured linen. Alec said, 'There's only one thing. The caterers still haven't arrived, so someone must stay behind to let them in, and it clearly can't be Sue or me.' I looked at Leonard expecting him to say, 'I'll stay.' No such luck. He returned my look with a glassy stare, and after an eternity of minutes I said, 'Off you go. I'll stay.' It's silly, but I still find it hard to forget that, on 12 August 1967, at the wedding of my closest and dearest friend, Leonard and not I was the witness. At the time, I was so furious that during the party afterwards, to make sure he wasn't in my eyeline, I retreated into the kitchen with John Osborne, who gossiped to me while I rinsed plates and glasses that needed returning to the fray. One incident went some way towards restoring my humour. A good-looking grey-haired woman joined us, first to ask for a large serving dish which I found for her, then to get a jug for iced water which I found for her too, then for an extra-large serving spoon, which I also produced. At her third and last visit she said, 'I'm Sue's mother. You seem to know this kitchen remarkably well?' I murmured something about small kitchens having not many hiding places and hoped she would leave it at that. Instead, she turned to John and said, 'And you, young man, what is your name?' John looked slightly nonplussed and replied, 'Oh, I'm sorry. I should have introduced myself. My name is John Osborne.' Veronica, for such was her name, retreated without a word, as though she'd just come face to face with the devil. John shrugged, turned to me and said, 'Well, I couldn't very well say I was Arnold Wesker.'

A short time later Paul Mills, then the director of MGM publicity, rang me to see if I was interested in working on *Alfred the Great*, to be directed by Clive Donner. Paul said, 'You're not the only designer they're considering, but I want to know if you'd like to do it?' It was a part of English history about which I knew nothing except the burning of the cakes, so I rushed to look up all the references I could, then quickly got on the telephone to the cautious and caring Pat Chard, my agent, to tell her what I knew and ask her what she thought. What I didn't say was that my reasons for wanting to do the film were personal rather than professional. Eight months in Ireland, where it was to be made, sounded exactly the period I needed away from Leonard and Namia. I would come out the other end refreshed and able to lead my own life, free of everyone and free of guilt.

Pat warned me that the film would have a huge cast and be a very heavy one indeed for a designer. But she said, 'Don't go out, I'll get straight on to Clive Donner.' She rang back in minutes with an appointment for that afternoon. Although I knew his work, the only film of his I'd seen was *The Caretaker*, which was, I thought, flawless.

XVI

Later that afternoon I presented myself at Wigmore Street where Clive Donner and his production designer, Michael Stringer, were waiting for me. They were both immediately friendly. I asked a few of the traditional questions like, 'Who's playing Alfred?' and 'May I read the script?' At the end of half an hour Clive said, 'If you want to do it, it's yours.' Then and there I said yes, and rushed home to ring Vangie Harrison and tell her we were back in business. Since *The Bliss of Mrs Blossom* and *Interlude* Vangie had remained my assistant and close friend.

So began our long and absorbing research into the ninth century, Anglo-Saxons and Vikings. Together we bought every reference book we could find, and thoroughly digested them. While we worked away on these, Clive's film *Here We Go Round the Mulberry Bush* opened, and immediately after the première he said, 'We are taking off for a long holiday in the sun.' I didn't discover until much later who 'we' was.

There is very little illustrated source material available on the Anglo Saxons, but a great many written and descriptive passages from early letters, diaries and manuscripts. Among these I especially liked Saint Aldhelm's tract in praise of virginity, which he sent to the nuns of Barking instructing them in the best way of life and mentioning contemporary practices which they should shun:

Satin underclothing, blue and violet, scarlet tunics with hoods, sleeves with silk stripes, shoes edged with red fur, hair carefully arrayed on forehead and temples with the curling iron – this is the modern habit. Dark veils yield to headdresses white and coloured, sewn with long ribbons and hanging to the ground, fingernails are sharpened like the talons of hawks or owls seeking their prey.

It is also said that the vice of drunkenness is far too common in your parishes. ... This is an evil peculiar to the heathen and to our race, for neither the Franks, nor the Gauls, nor the Lombards, nor the Romans, nor the Greeks practise it. ...

In the film the Vikings were to be shown as more highly trained and disciplined fighters than the Saxons, as indeed they were; and in order to solve the difficulty of the audience being able to differentiate between the two sides in a battle, we intended to dress the Viking army in dark steely blue and the Saxons in natural earth colours, as if they had run to battle straight from their farms.

No one before had tried to do a film of the period with any degree of authenticity, and we needed every minute of the six to eight pre-production months. The Vikings, stylized into a uniform armour, were not nearly such a problem as the Saxons, with few if any visual references available. I read as much as I could find about their customs and the way they lived, the people with whom they traded, the fabrics and dyes they used. Finally it all came down to just two sources of reference on which to base their costumes. We decided that of these two the Bayeux tapestries were too late, but that the source material from Byzantium, while minimally too early, was a wiser choice. The simplicity of the secular clothes in the ninth century, the ecclesiastical detail in Byzantine mosaics, and the few early linear illustrations in Anglo-Saxon manuscripts, gave us a line to follow.

The clothes of the rich Saxon nobles were made of silk, linen, wool or velvet, often decorated with gold or silver thread. Their jewellery was sophisticated and very beautiful: foil-backed stones set in gold, shoulder clasps of silver or gold manufactured by prisoners of war brought to England from North Africa.

The peasants dressed in cotton or rough wool. Unmarried girls left their hair loose, married women put it up, and covered their heads with a hood which combined with a cowl to cover their necks. Because gloves were known only to aristocratic falconers, the immensely long sleeves of the peasants, which reached from shoulder to floor, were in winter wound round and round their hands to keep them warm.

Those were our basic rules when the time came for us to get on with looking for fabrics, and to experiment with different methods of dyeing them. Throughout the film, Alex Thompson, the lighting cameraman, was to use a blue filter, which, though it gives the skin a marvellous creamy texture and takes the emerald curse off the green Irish grass, meant that we had to take extreme care with our reds, or they would appear hideously garish.

The sheer numbers, two thousand on the battlefield at one time, were a headache not only for the wardrobe staff, but also for make-up, hairdressers, and the prop department who had to face the problem of, when the time came, issuing immense quantities of side arms, fighting knives, and shields. Bermans were anxious to make the helmets of heavy gelatinous rubber but I said a categorical no. I'd seen too many bounce across film battlefields like footballs.

When Clive and 'we' returned from holiday, Vangie and I showed him our drawings and started having costumes for the principals made, also prototypes of Viking armour, fibreglass helmets, and padded and studded leather armour for the Saxon nobles. We bought calf skins, goat skins and rabbit skins, ranging in colour from gleaming soft black fur to pale creamy white. In a strange biblical shop in Bloomsbury we bought for £200 enough embroidery – incredibly fine silk worked on linen – to embellish all the Court costumes. To have had it made would have run into thousands of pounds.

Eventually, there was nothing left to do in London and the whole giant caravan set off for Galway. Clive had already been there rehearsing for two weeks with David Hemmings, Michael York, Colin Blakely, Prunella Ransome, Sinead Cusack, Ian McKellen and Vivien Merchant. My greatest misery was having to leave Vangie behind. She'd become like an extension to my right arm. But her children were too young to be left for so long. Instead, Ann Gainsford, who had been working on the hand props and jewellery, came with me and turned out to be a staunch and witty assistant. Trained in Italy on many of Franco Zeffirelli's productions, and with a degree in history from Oxford, she was not about to be fased by anything.

Ann, Jo Knowles, the continuity girl, and I took a perfectly hideous bijou bungalow together, but it was big enough for us not to be sitting on top of each other, and much more peaceful than an hotel.

Clive had taken Kilcolgan Castle, a miniature Strawberry Hill Gothic manor, with salmon leaping almost onto the front lawn, and all the milk and butter tasting of the wild garlic the cows grazed on.

Fred Brazier, a fragile-looking man with the strength of Samson, who superbly co-ordinated Bermans' side of things while we were on location, joined me for dinner with Clive the night of our arrival. After a certain amount of indiscreet questioning I discovered that 'we', who wasn't there, was in fact Penelope Mortimer, with whom he'd been having an on-and-off affair for some years. She had originally planned to stay in Galway for the whole of the shooting schedule, because she believed it would be a calm place in which to write her new novel, but it proved too grey, so she stayed only a few days and left before my arrival.

Clive would often ask me to dine during those early weeks, but the wardrobe staff were so busy and working so late that I felt I should be with them. Then one day when he and I were in Prunella Ransome's caravan discussing some detail or other, Prunella was called to the telephone and Clive again said, 'Come to dinner tonight.... No one else is coming.' I said, 'Thank you. Yes,' while my inside gave a familiar lurch and I thought, Whoops, here I go again.

Film unit gossip, I believe, spreads from under the hair-dryers at a hairdresser's in the Fulham Road, and indeed no sooner were more of my clothes at Kilcolgan than at the bijou bungalow, when Clive received a telegram saying: 'Arriving Shannon 2.30 today – Love Penelope.' Clive showed me the telegram. All I could say was, 'Shit': I was wanted on the set, but my clothes, make-up and toothbrush needed to be moved in the hour and a half before Penelope was due to arrive. It was time to confide in Gerry, Clive's driver. He raced to Kilcolgan, came back with all my possessions, and then went off to Shannon to collect Penelope.

Neither Clive nor I had been discreet. As with most affairs that start well, we went about in an aura of glowing contentment, so the entire unit knew what was happening. Out of the corner of my eyes, concealed behind giant wrap-around dark glasses, I saw Penelope arrive. I was sitting in Clive's chair with his name stencilled on the back and I rose and walked in the opposite direction. Johnny Briggs, who was in charge of the men's wardrobe, moved to meet me. 'She knows. She hasn't taken her eyes off you since she arrived,' he said. 'Tough,' I said, 'I wonder how long she'll stay.' Later in the afternoon we were introduced, and both of us pretended we didn't remember meeting before at the Royal Court Theatre.

Vangie was arriving that weekend with her children, for which I thanked God. Apart from the fact that it took my mind off Penelope, it was a sheer joy to see her again, and kept me happily occupied until Clive was once more alone.

Penelope only made one other short visit during the rest of the Galway shooting, and once more there was boxing and coxing as Gerry moved my luggage out and hers in, keeping a perfectly innocent poker-face. Everyone else could joke about it, and everyone did, but not Gerry; his loyalty to Clive was total.

After Penelope's last stay Clive and I gave up any attempt to live apart, and even when his parents were there, or friends, or a whole tribe of cousins, or his doctor, I stayed on as part of the household.

I was working hard and getting to know Clive, who was different from any other man I had known. The one quality he shared with others was that of being an only child, like Freddie Ayer, John Osborne, Leonard Rosoman and Robert Namia. Lithe and swift both intellectually and physically, he has the capacity to think while on the run of several subjects simultaneously, and with total concentration on each. François Truffaut's depiction of a film director at the beginning of *Day for Night* could be a portrait of Clive. Extraordinarily decisive in thought and action, he dislikes feeling that he is being manipulated into a situation where he may feel trapped. He needs an area of space in which he can move freely and work without interference. He has a very rare sweetness of character which makes him understanding of the frailties of weaker persons, and this indulgence eventually results, perforce, in a culling of the lame ducks he manages to collect. At the age of fifteen he already knew where his future lay, and this is one of the very few qualities we share. He is infinitely gentler and more gregarious than I, who am one of nature's reclusive hermits, sitting in my kennel snapping at passers-by, and while Clive is actually interested in other people, I choose to bury my head in a book. Since he is neither tall nor short, my head fits neatly under his chin when we are both standing; his face is somewhere between square and rectangular and his nose, which is totally straight while mine can't even be called tip-tilted, just simply turned up, is what I most envy about him – that and his inexhaustible energy.

Meanwhile, I wasn't thinking about the future for a change, but enjoying the present – and working very hard. There was a lot going on. Because they were much easier to train in Dark Age combat than the men we were getting from the Galway Labour Exchange, about a thousand soldiers from the Irish Army had joined the cast, and some of them were trained by the stunt men until they became more than adequate stunt men themselves. Students from Dublin and Galway Universities were also useful in an endless number of small parts, providing one could prise the copies of Eisenstein from under their arms before the cameras turned.

Every morning, like sergeants on a parade ground, the whole wardrobe staff would go along the ranks of men inspecting them to see if they were properly dressed. The Irish love their cloth caps even better than poteen. They would rather nail them to their heads than take them off, and many a small tweed frill was found peeping from under the edge of a Viking helmet. It's not that they mind how many clothes, or layers of clothes, they are asked to put on; what they can't bear is having to remove anything.

The all-night shooting of the Battle of Ashdown in a long deep valley where Queen Maeve is said to have lived, enclosed on either side by gnarled and twisted trees, was – for me at least – especially marvellous. We stopped at first light, as the sky was getting pearly pale, and glancing down I discovered I was walking through a carpet of sweet scented multi-coloured wild orchids, thickly clustered and stretching as far as I could see. On the other hand, the Battle of Athelney was a nightmare. To walk on the battleground, a flat expanse of moving bog, was like walking on an oversprung, waterlogged dance floor. The weather was appalling and all the trees had been cut down, so there was no shelter. At the end of the shooting, something made me lift one of the stunted bushes scattered around and under it I found a helmet, a beard and a wig. I went on and lifted another, and this time discovered a cloak, a shield and a helmet. All over the battlefield, strewn it seemed under every available twig, were props and bits of costume that, during the day, people had grown tired of carrying. The prop men did a tour of the field and, when they returned, their truck was laden.

About this time I developed a raging temperature. If I bent over I thought my head would fall off, but the work had to be done. I was trying to create a great blazing fireball of colourful costumes around Alfred at the middle of the Saxon phalanx. When the job was finally over, I sent a message to Clive saying I'd got flu and thought he would be better off if I went back to the bijou residence for the night. But as I was about to set off with Barbara Gillette, a friend from past films who ran the women's wardrobe, the rain began to come down in torrents. The wardrobe Dormobile was parked beside us so we clambered in. To my amazement Barbara locked the door and then proceeded to give me 'a piece of her mind', 'a good talking to', 'a lecture more in sorrow than in anger'. She said, 'You are no longer the Jocelyn I know and have worked with. On this film you have spent your time socializing with the director.' I said, 'Barbara, if you mean fucking, be brave enough to say so, because a social life is *not* what I'm having.'

On and on she went. My head ached as though every word was being hammered into it. The lecture – it wasn't a conversation – went on for three-quarters of an hour until I frigidly said I was sorry I hadn't lived up to her expectations, but I was off to bed; the film was nearly over, and she wouldn't have to put up with me for much longer and had better just grin and bear it.

I'm still astonished that all this happened, except that Barbara and I did not see eye-to-eye in our work. Films being as volatile as they are, I always at least try to be prepared and ready to cope with any change of schedule at any time. But in Barbara's rule book – and she did run her department immaculately – if the wardrobe always said 'Yes, of course we can', it appeared weak, and weak it would only appear over her dead body. Her method of running a wardrobe perfectly was to be firm, mine – possibly I had worked too often with the very practical French – was to be flexible, and because we remained incapable of seeing each other's point of view, this degenerated into a power struggle between us. It was a breached friendship I have never been able to heal.

The filming of *Alfred* drew to an end. The winding-down process is always the same. First the big crowds go, then the small-part actors are sent home; finally, one day, all that is left are the director, the camera crew, wardrobe, make-up, hairdressing, and perhaps an actor or two. In this case it was David Hemmings who was needed for a whole series of close-up linking shots to be cut in between different

120

episodes in the film: fifteen close-ups, fifteen changes of hair, make-up and costume, and that was that. We had all been in Galway for nearly nine months. It was time to go back to London and face reality.

Clive was looking exhausted and wanted a complete rest before he started editing. At my suggestion letters and cables were sent to the Centre Culturel-Hammamet. Once they had received the whole lot, and run their fingers over the letter heading, they wrote back to say that although they were officially closed for their yearly repaint, they would be delighted to receive him if he wouldn't be too bored there by himself with only a staff of servants. It was exactly what he needed. Very tentatively I said, 'If you do get lonely, let me know and I'll come. But if I do, be prepared to be cited as correspondent by Leonard.'

When I arrived in London the studio was deserted, for Leonard was in Spain, though due back. Clive left for Tunis next day. Twenty-four hours later Leonard returned looking much better than when I'd last seen him. We sat down amiably to have a drink and I said, 'Tell me truthfully Leonard, haven't you been better off and happier without me?'

'Well, to be truthful, if you hadn't brought it up, I was going to – yes, I have.'

So far so very easy and good. I said it was absolutely up to him: if he wanted to divorce me, I would give him the evidence; if he didn't, that was all right too.

No! No! a divorce it must be.

'Well,' I said, 'that's all right then. I only stayed in London to have this talk with you. I'm off to North Africa on Saturday, I need a holiday.'

'With Namia?'

'No,' I replied bluntly, 'with Clive Donner.'

Leonard's face became flintier, the nose lengthened, the lips disappeared altogether and he turned on me scornfully. I'd unthinkingly hurt his pride. Scorn and rage rained down on my head. In his eyes I was the whore of Babylon and, what's more, all his friends thought so too.

I was so thankful that on the flight to Tunis some friends were travelling in the same plane. I felt as thought my guts had been kicked in by a draught-horse, and at half hourly intervals I had to rush to the lavatory – one end or the other was acting up. Given the sight of Clive at Tunis airport, I understood how Christ felt when he ran into John the Baptist after forty days and forty nights in the wilderness.

We arrived in Hammamet and Clive said, 'I changed rooms this morning – they gave me the choice of anywhere and I decided you would like this one best.' We made our way along a path between olives and oranges and lemons to the little Arab villa I had shared with Leonard two years earlier, in 1965. I had no feelings of guilt about lying in the same bed as I had with Leonard; that holiday was past and its memories were made up of John Cranko and Robert Namia rather than Leonard. In the freshly painted villa, with my favourite double datura blooming against the wall, I felt protected and cared for. Clive's re-silience is like that of a child, and after the few days he'd already spent in the sun, he looked healthy, sunburned and clear-eyed. I had a prison pallor, was shaking like a leaf, and it took all his calm to quieten me down.

Next morning while I was lying half-awake after a perfect night's sleep there was a knock on the door and in came Abu el Salim with orange juice, fresh figs and coffee. 'Why, it's you, Madame,' he said. 'Monsieur very lonely by himself.'

With the whole place empty, Clive and I were able to explore every inch as slowly as we wished. I pointed out to him the curiously sinister house beyond the walls of the Centre which belonged to a male and female English homosexual couple. John Cranko and I had gone there to tea on my previous visit. Running freely through it were fowls, large and small, from peacocks to small, tatty white birds with elaborate feathered anklets like pie frills. For some reason the house had seemed to embrace a total decadence I'd never experienced before. All the rooms smelled of stale alcohol. Tea was taken in the garden. I was con-vinced it was laced with LSD, and John Cranko and I had sat together on a rock holding each other's hands so tightly it's a wonder we didn't cut off our blood circulation. The next morning John came in after break-fast and said, 'You know x who is a house guest next door?'

'Yes. Why?'

'Last night he got drunk and went down to walk on the beach. While there he met a ravishing Arab boy and they retired into the sand dunes together. x woke as dawn was breaking, cold and stark naked, nothing left, nothing, his clothes, his watch, his underclothes all gone. He had to creep back to Horror House like that and is now sleeping off shame and a hangover on the beach.'

No such dramas filled the days I spent there with Clive. We would breakfast, make our leisurely way to the all-but-deserted beach, and wander back to the house at lunchtime for bread, cheese and fruit served on a tray in the garden. After a siesta, we returned to the beach at about five for a favourite moment, which was when a camel train, starting at the very farthest end of the beach, slowly and silently made its way home, caparisoned like the Queen of Sheba's cortège, with bridles and saddlecloths embroidered in richly coloured wools. It was a sight of which I never grew tired. Equally fascinating was to walk along the beach towards Hammamet about midday and see the village women cooling off in the shallow water, with all their layers of skirts and veils floating about them like multi-coloured seaweed as they gently bounced up and down in the sea.

All too soon we were back in London, Clive coming into my studio in Roland Gardens for a drink before going on to his own flat in Weymouth Street. The studio, my bolt hole, was shining, clean and welcoming, albeit a little austere as I'd never actually lived in it, but only worked there. Even after Clive had left I felt happy and peaceful – more so when, about an hour later, he rang and said, 'Let's have dinner together.'

During the next few weeks I moved completely out of Leonard's place at Pembroke Studios and into Roland Gardens, taking with me some treasured possessions, among them an English seventeenth-century provincial desk, a cane chair that had come from Queen Mary's gazebo at Marlborough House, and an early butcher's table. In under a month Roland Gardens was totally equipped for working *and* living, and it fitted round me as snugly as a carapace.

Before that happy state was achieved, and after our dinner together, Clive went to Cornwall for a short stay with Ken Taylor, the scriptwriter of *Alfred*. I was occupied less pleasantly, spending a great deal of time in a dentist's chair having a root canal filling done. At the start of the following weekend I was wakened by that relentless nagging pain which means all is far from well and, indeed, an abscess had formed. My teeth, which initially looked like a string of even, lustrous pearls, now had the consistency of biscuits, like those of most Australians who grew up before discovering just how deficient the water in that country is in calcium and sulphur. I'd even managed to break a tooth on a soft-boiled egg and another eating a ripe avocado pear. There was no way I was going to trust my present trouble to a dental hospital, nor could I trace my own dentist, Geoffrey Simpson, because he'd vanished for the weekend out of London. I have, luckily, a very high threshold of pain, so I decided I would stick it out until Monday morning. But by then I had a face like Quasimodo. Unlike most abscesses, which either swell or hurt, this was doing both, and the whole of the left side of my face was dragged out of alignment – my eye was where my cheekbone should have been, and the corner of my mouth was on my jaw bone.

At eight-thirty, shrouded in scarves and dark glasses, and without even bothering to telephone for an appointment, I made my way to Harley Street. Geoffrey Simpson wasn't there; he'd developed pneumonia over the weekend. His partner backed away as though I had leprosy, and his nurse telephoned every dental surgeon in London until she found one who could deal with an emergency quickly. I was laid out with pentathol, and the offending tooth was carefully removed. Vangie was telephoned and asked to collect me, put me to bed, and keep me there for two days. During that time she was kindness itself, slipping in and out like a beneficent ghost to see that I was all right; I would wake up and then nod off again.

Late on Wednesday afternoon, the telephone rang. I put out a feeble hand to pick it up and heard crackle ... word ... crackle, as though someone was speaking from the moon. I said, 'I can't hear you and anyway I'm coming out of an anaesthetic,' and put the receiver back in place. Ten minutes later it rang again, and a determined, clarion voice said, 'My name is Roy Stevens. I am telephoning for David Lean. Could you come to Ireland and meet him?'

'No,' I said ungraciously, 'I've just been to Ireland.' Then I added, 'What's the film?' It's that deadly curiosity that snares one every time. I'd shown enough interest for it to be worth their while sending a script, which arrived with a letter that evening. It weighed a ton in my hand. I laid it beside my bed and went back to sleep until the morning. After eighteen hours' sleep I felt human again, even if I still looked a mess and, after bathing, I picked up the Bible-sized script.

On the bright blue cover of the script I read: '*Ryan's Daughter* – an original screenplay by Robert Bolt.' Roy Stevens's letter told me it was to be produced for MGM by Anthony Havelock-Allen and directed by David Lean, with Sarah Miles in the title role of Rosy and Robert Mitchum as the schoolteacher whom she marries. I knew Sarah from *Blow-Up*; she had been living with Robert Bolt, but now they were married with a son called Thomas. The script captivated me. Set in 1916 in the time of Michael Collins and 'the Troubles', the whole action took place in a small Irish village on the Dingle Peninsula.

That night, Clive was due back from Cornwall. When he arrived I put the script in his hands and asked, 'What shall I do?' Clive had worked in the cutting rooms for several years as David Lean's assistant. He had been close to him, had learned from him, and greatly admired him. He said, 'It's a chance you'll bitterly regret if you don't take it.'

In the morning I telephoned Roy Stevens, and it was arranged that I should fly to Cork next day, a Wednesday, talk with David Lean and Stephen Grimes, the production designer, and then we would make up our minds if we could work together. Clive said he would meet me in Dublin on the Friday evening, and we planned to drive to Galway and spend a nostalgic weekend lunching at Paddy Moran's oyster bar and dining at the Tavern.

The plane landed at Cork and I was off in seconds with the barest amount of hand luggage, and not knowing who on earth to look for. Somebody came up behind me, lifted me off the ground, swirled me round and placed me carefully back on the ground again. It was Gerry, Clive's driver, now driving for David Lean. We chattered like monkeys all the way to Killarney, where Gerry dropped me at the hotel and gave me David's room number to call.

I had no preconceived idea about David Lean at all. We spoke and agreed to meet for tea in his suite in about half an hour. I arrived to be greeted by a tall, grey haired man, sunburned, friendly with a certain shyness in his manner, pale blue eyes and regular, extremely handsome features. He wore grey trousers, a white cotton polo-necked pullover and a navy blue cashmere cardigan. This, it turned out, was his working uniform, and he put on an immaculately fresh version of it every day we were shooting, so that he always looked the same unless it was raining, when he would add a raincoat.

I looked round the room for any personal object that might tell me something about him, but all I could see was a pair of women's low-heeled black patent leather shoes and a record player. We talked about the script and the characters – by now John Mills had agreed to play the village idiot, and Trevor Howard the parish priest. I suggested that village people of that period in Ireland would appear up to fifty years behind the contemporary fashion: hems to the ground, collars boned, and probably an abundance of Irish lace trimming both collars and cuffs, with old women looking like black beetles in black shoes and stockings, shawls and headscarves. The young girls would put their hair up only once they were married, hair going up as hems came down.

Later Stephen Grimes came in, a tall bearded man, very nice, very softly spoken. Soon the owner of the black patent leather shoes arrived too. She and David had eloped earlier in 1968 from her parents' hotel in India without taking even a toothbrush with them. Later she became his wife. Tall and supple, Sandy was a little like a pre-Renaissance Madonna, with pale honey-coloured hair, a high forehead and long, delicately rounded limbs. She seemed half-girl, half-woman, was utterly in love with David and, fresh from her convent education, waiting for everything that he could teach her about life, film-making, growing up, living and loving. Eventually, in 1986 they fell out of love and parted.

Over those few days in Killarney, getting to know David and his colleagues, I could sense the hyper-perfectionist that he is, and I liked him. After working with many extreme extroverts, I found him by

126

comparison quiet, almost inarticulate, but very sure of what he wanted. So I had a light heart when Gerry drove me to Dublin to meet Clive.

We spent the night there and then motored to Galway, passing at Athlone the two Viking boats we'd used during the shooting of *Alfred*, which were still anchored there. No sooner had we shown our noses in Galway than every second passer-by, or so it seemed, stopped us in the street to ask if we were returning to make another 'fillum', or when, indeed, they would have a chance to see the first 'fillum'.

Back to London meant back to the cutting-room for Clive, and for me back to the drawing board. Happily, Vangie had taken over from me a Peter Sellers film, *The Magic Christian*, that I'd just started work on. Despite my verbal commitment to it, its producer, Denis O'Dell, had said with huge generosity, 'No one owes us that kind of loyalty, and anyway Vangie can do it just as well as you, can't you Vangie?' Vangie agreed that she'd like to try, so all was satisfactorily resolved, except that I was to be deprived of a trusted and talented assistant.

I left *The Magic Christian* without saying goodbye to Peter Sellers, though I did see him once more, years afterwards, just before he died, at a time when Clive had agreed to direct the next Clouseau film for him. I never knew Peter well, but during the pre-production days of *The Magic Christian* we had met quite often in his dim apartment in Half Moon Street, with its walls of gloomy antiqued mirror and drawn curtains. This was a bad period during one of his marriages: he was always hiding behind dark glasses, amiable but not communicative, and a general air of gloom used to hang over the meetings. I was, in fact, dreading the film and used to heave a sigh of relief once we got outside.

Meeting him again much later at his home in Switzerland with Clive was altogether different. They were friends, had worked together before, notably on *What's New Pussycat?*, and shared a delight in each other's wit. But I was shocked then by Peter's physical appearance. He looked very thin and frail and, against all doctors' advice, had just undergone intense cosmetic surgery. His neck had a row of minute, faintly visible pintucks in it to take up the slack skin, and he was still convalescent from the operation, so he tired easily. However, he and Clive accomplished all they needed to at that stage, and we all returned to London in high spirits, flying back in Peter's tiny plane. My last sight of him came as his 'limo' passed ours on the road from the airport. He gave us a gracious Royal wave. The next day he was dead.

My immediate problem with *Ryan's Daughter* was to find a replacement for Vangie. Ruth Myers, who had managed to cope skilfully with *The Sailor From Gibraltar* after I left, and went on to work on her own after assisting Jocelyn Herbert with the costume designs for Karel Reisz's *Isadora*, had recently married John Heilpern, an *Observer* feature writer. Now, once again, she came up trumps. She was pregnant and didn't feel she could take on a production of her own, but very much wanted to come and work with me again.

Then came the always difficult subject of wardrobe staff. Johnny Briggs, though not overwhelmed at the prospect of another long spell in Ireland, eventually said yes; and Bermans found for me a pretty young girl called Diane Jones, who came multi-recommended. I couldn't believe my luck.

Starting the real work, I drew for Sarah Miles every combination of skirt and blouse, period dress, wedding dress, shoes, underclothes and nightdress, and I pinned to each several choices of fabric. When Ruth and I took them to David Lean at the Ritz, he loved them all. What no one had told me was that he couldn't read a costume drawing. I might as well have shown him blank sheets of paper. Stephen Grimes said later that he always got David to initial every set design sketch he approved. I don't think that would have helped me, though. A lot of the drawings of mine that he'd liked clearly wouldn't have produced the clothes he had locked somewhere in his mind but was incapable of describing to me. This meant that we had to make a series of alternatives for him to choose from. I had asked him to a fitting with Sarah, but he was in London for too short a time. In the end, all the clothes had to be finished and despatched to Ireland without his setting eyes on any of them.

The natural outcome of this was several months of very tricky negotiation between us. I'm certain he was wishing that he had engaged Phyllis Dalton, who had done so triumphantly well for him on both *Lawrence of Arabia* and *Doctor Zhivago*, and I certainly wished she were there instead of me. It got to the point where nothing I did pleased him. This was aggravated, if anything, by Robert Mitchum coming to my rescue and telling him that he didn't deserve such a talented, hard-working designer anyway, and why didn't he pull himself together to try to help rather than hinder me.

I woke up in despair one morning and went to the wardrobe before anyone else was stirring to draft a letter of resignation. In mid-sentence, Josie MacAvin, Stephen's assistant and set-dresser, came in to borrow something: 'What are you doing here at this ungodly hour?'

'Resigning.'

'Does Stephen know?'

'I don't see how he can, I haven't seen him this morning.'

Josie didn't wait. I chased her out into Dingle's main street, but the tail of her car had already disappeared, and Stephen himself appeared in less than an hour. 'Well?' he said. I handed him the draft letter. He read it, put it down and said, 'I agree with every word you say, but please, for my sake, don't do it.'

'What's the point of working one's guts out to please a man who's determined to be displeased?' I asked. 'Above all, there's no pleasure in working under that degree of anxiety.'

'Don't do anything before tonight's fittings. You know he'll never apologize, don't you?'

'I don't want an apology, I just want out. I won't deliver the letter before tonight, but if tonight is a repetition of every other night, it will be much more unpleasant, because I'll just say what I think in front of Robert, Sarah, the wardrobe staff, and whoever else happens to be around – OK?'

'Yes, OK,' said Stephen. 'Anyway, it's more dignified.' I very much doubted that.

This time the costume in dispute was what Rosy would wear for her assignation with the English officer; what she would feel was right and proper for a 'lady's riding habit'. We'd arranged for her horse to be brought to the open ground at the back of the wardrobe so that David could see horse and rider as one.

I'd really gone over the top. The first choice was a beige skirt with a silk taffeta petticoat and a Liberty lawn blouse with a high collar and a shawl. The second offering was a dark green riding skirt over a crimson silk taffeta flounced petticoat, a vermilion blouse with matching silk scarf, a heavy fringed black chenille shawl and an old black bowler hat. There was a third choice, but I've mercifully forgotten what it was. In

129

the event, David chose the second costume, which I felt unsuitable because the cost of the taffeta petticoat would have been beyond the purse of Sarah's character in Ireland at the time; also the blouse originally had a period cut and collar, but David wanted it to open down the front, which made it look like an expensive modern shirt. He was probably dramatically right – she looked marvellous on screen – but it goes against the grain with any designer to be so flagrantly out of period in a period film; it enters the realms of fantasy.

Sarah's fitting had by now become a nightly cabaret for the higher echelons of the unit, so everyone trooped in after shooting, clamouring for drinks to warm them. I'd got past caring. David arrived. I said, 'We've got several things to show you. You may feel I've gone too far.'

Sarah went out to mount the horse and ride past the production office windows. Meanwhile a certain amount of coming and going and drink pouring was going on. David turned to me: 'Jocelyn, I owe you an apology.' This was said in front of his assembled troops. I was so astonished that my mouth hung indelicately open for seconds before I was able to respond in any way. The rug had been pulled from under my feet, and I knew I would now stay with the film for as long as I was needed. It didn't occur to me that Stephen had skilfully stage-managed the whole scene, and only years later did he tell me. But I'm glad he did, because once David and I got onto an even keel I found him fascinating and rewarding to work with.

The main Irish actors came from Dublin, a lot of them were Abbey Players; the crowd we recruited from the surrounding villages, and the children from local schools. They were each given costumes that, with additions and subtractions, would do for spring, summer, autumn and winter; and we had to be prepared at all times to take advantage of any change in the weather. There was no way of accurately forecasting this because we were in such a curious and isolated geographical position, on a peninsula jutting into the Atlantic, with a range of mountains between us and the rest of Ireland. The production office would telephone the Met office for a forecast. They would answer, 'What's it look like there?' We would all hang out of the window and relay to Roy Stevens what we could see, which he in turn would tell them, and they would say, 'Ah, well that's most likely how it'll be all day.' In the end, it proved impossible to produce a normal call sheet listing the scenes to be shot next day, so every morning we were issued instead with one giving no less than five alternative weather calls. This meant that we had to go everywhere with one giant wardrobe van equipped to shoot in five different locations with five different sets of actors.

I had, though, one lovely luxury: my own car and driver, Mossy, chosen by me because, apart from Gerry, he was the only Irish driver I could understand. He was an endlessly kind and willing man, and once I'd taught him not to talk to me too much in the car because that was where I did most of my thinking and problem solving, he was absolutely perfect except for one habit I could never break. If I was sitting in the back and asked him a question like, 'Is that tiny stone hut really the Gallaurus Oratory?' to answer he would keep on driving but with his head turned totally round, so that he could look at me. In vain would I scream, 'Mossy, for God's sake keep your eyes on the road.'

'No, Miss Jocelyn, that would be most impolite of me.'

'Better alive and rude than dead through politeness,' I kept saying. No good. So I learned to sit in the front if I wanted conversation, and in the back if I wanted silence.

Among those in the cast engaged from Dublin was an actress who had an unbelievably beautiful black cloak with an enormous full hood. It looked to be a perfect eighteenth-century design, and such it turned out to be, of the kind traditionally worn in Kinsale. I asked her if she would mind wearing it in the film, and she readily agreed because in cold weather she could pile black pullovers on under it, or just as easily shed them when it was warmer. But I, having seen it, wanted more of these rare and wonderful cloaks.

With great good luck a tinker with a horse and cart had, at about this time, come into my life. He would sometimes arrive laden with goodies, like a nineteenth-century grey alpaca dress still with its basting thread in it, children's boots, or dark plaid shawls. So I waited keenly for the next sight of his jolly sinful red face, mop of black hair, and only alternate teeth.

'Would there be anytink you'd be wantin', laydee?' he asked winningly when I saw him again, for we'd bargain in the street like Arabs.

'Yes, nine Kinsale cloaks. Do you think you can find them for me?'

'Yes, wot you tink of paying?'

'Ten pounds each, cross my heart,' I said. Before setting off, he actually made me cross my heart, believing by now, it seemed, that I was some sort of female anti-Christ. I thought, oh well, that's the last of him. Two weeks later I was in the main wardrobe and heard Johnny Briggs calling me: 'Jocelyn, come on, your friend's back.' I went out to see not nine but thirteen Kinsale cloaks, some in rags and tatters, some green with age, but all the better for that. I went through them, and hated myself for saying, 'Ninety pounds for nine; I don't believe you'll be losing if I pay you ninety pounds for all thirteen.'

'Oh, you'd be an 'ard woman to bargain wit',' he said.

'Well, convince me you won't be making a handsome profit?'

'I can't,' he said. 'Some I got for nuttin'.'

So I gave him ninety pounds sterling, he gave me thirteen cloaks, and I left Johnny, who is softer than I am, to buy the rest of his loot on more generous terms. That way I felt things balanced.

We used the Kinsale cloaks for the scene where Sarah's hair was pulled out and her clothes torn by a group of vulture-like village harpies. One really good cloak, a virtual museum piece, I kept and brought back to London for Vangie.

There were two surprises for me during the film: one pleasant, the other not. The pleasant surprise was Robert Mitchum, whom I found to be the least vain and most delightfully intelligent of actors. He arrived for his first fitting straight from an eleven-hour flight from Los Angeles. All Bermans' staff were hanging out the windows to look at him as he got out of a black Rolls, so by the time I got to the fitting room I had already been told that he was wearing a suntan, a black hat, dark glasses, black trousers, a black polo-necked pullover, black socks, black shoes, a black raincoat and, round his neck, a long thick gold chain. I introduced myself and Ruth and we started the fittings: suits, shirts, collars, nightshirts, an unlined grey alpaca jacket for teaching in, a raincoat and a tweed coat. As things progressed we talked. I answered his questions about the location, the other actors, the crew. Throughout the entire session he'd had his back to the mirror and was turned towards me. I finally said, 'Don't you want to look at yourself?' he replied, 'No, I figure you know what you're doing; no sense in my interfering; everything's comfortable.' I was dedicated to him from that moment on, and he remained my defender and ally. I seldom see him, but continue to think of him as a true friend.

The less pleasant surprise was the crowd fittings. I went to the first one having sprayed myself from head to foot with insecticide and holding in my hand a bunch of Kleenex soaked in Diorissima. At the end of the day, no doubt due to these precautions, I was bite free, thank God, but Diane Jones, Johnny Briggs, and their Irish assistants looked as though they had German measles. Every twenty-four hours the marquees where the crowd clothes hung each night were fumigated. But we fought a losing battle: the fleas bred faster than we could kill them. I do believe our Irish crowd, all raised from nearby villages, were inured against such pests, for they never complained. It seemed to be only British blood the fleas chose to suck on. Ultimately, the smell in the marquees became so bad despite my scented tissues I insisted on doing the fittings outside.

Meanwhile, returning to London for the première of *Alfred*, I had ten marvellous days with Clive, whom I hadn't seen for eight months. Ruth Myers collected me at the airport, back to her normal size, and with a huge baby daughter. I was shy of seeing Clive again after what seemed an eternity, though we'd been constantly in touch, writing and telephoning. But it was a shyness that vanished in an instant, and it comforted me that when it was time to go back to Dingle it wasn't for long, because there was very little left for me to do there, apart from showing David and Sarah, for decision, three costumes I was having made while I was with Clive in London.

One of these they were to choose for Sarah in a very special scene where she and Christopher Jones, the British officer, walk along a sunlit beach together. I thought of it as a dream sequence, he in full dress uniform and she – though I'd kept yellow out of every frame of the film so far – in sulphur yellow chiffon. This, against the pale sand and washed-out blue of sea and sky, would give visual bite to the scene. I was anxious that David and Sarah should agree.

They were shooting on the beach when I arrived back, and Sarah was in her caravan waiting to try the clothes on. Stephen and I had privately decided to leave the alternatives aside and to go all out for the yellow dress. Quickly we got Sarah into it. She looked ravishing. A wide satin ribbon decorated with white silk roses circled her waist, she wore a lavender grey hat piled high with more silk roses, and carried a lavender grey parasol. David was enchanted. It was the only dress that he really fell for, and the one that was featured on all the posters and in all the publicity. At last I felt totally vindicated.

Always on a film there is one costume I choose to make myself. No matter what it is, it always remains for me not the best designed and certainly not the best made, but my favourite of the whole production. On *Ryan's Daughter* I decorated John Mills's wedding suit. I spent hours breaking it down, sewing it back together again, and attaching small broken brooches of glass and tin to it though they scarcely registered. Finally, just before the wedding scene was shot, I placed an enormous daffodil in his buttonhole. But weeks later, when we had to do pick-up shots of the party following the wedding, daffodils had finished blooming. By some miracle I'd measured the original, and the art department came up with an artificial one exactly the same size. Even Phyll Crocker, the hawk-eyed continuity girl, didn't question its authenticity.

By this time David had shot on every costume for every season of the year, and I felt I was redundant. Each morning I would go into the production office and say, 'Why can't I go home?' Each day Roy Stevens would say, 'Because we might need you.' After eight weeks of this same dialogue, I found him looking worried. Weather hold-ups were costing money and I said, 'What will you do?' Without thinking, he said, 'Start pulling out people who aren't essential.'

'Me first?'

Roy looked at me, thought a bit, and said, 'You won't start immediately on another film if I let you go?'

'Start on another film, you must be mad. I just want a long lie down.'

'All right,' he said, 'You can go in two days if David agrees, but only if you'll come back if we need you.'

'Of course I'll come back if I'm needed, but I won't be.'

Two days later I was packed and airborne for London. It was October and I had been working on *Ryan's Daughter* for part of 1967 and almost the whole of 1968. But when I got back to Roland Gardens it occurred to me that no matter how much one longs for home, there is always, once you are there, a tremendous feeling of let-down, of being in a vacuum, after so many months away, collaborating so closely with other people in a close-knit microcosm. This time however, the feeling came only after a long sleep.

During October it was freezing cold and the mother of one of Clive's closest friends, Michael Birkett, died from virus influenza. The widow of the Nuremberg trial judge, Norman Birkett, Lady Birkett had moved on her husband's death seven years earlier from their large house in Chalfont to a smaller but charming flint and brick house with almost three acres of garden, right on top of a ridge of the

Chilterns just outside the village of Speen. It was a house Clive had fallen in love with at first sight. He talked to Michael, discovered he wanted to sell, so took me to look at it. It was a perfect small country house that had once been two adjoining cottages. The drawing-room had the original farmhouse fireplace and bread oven, and one huge window that looked over the valley. A glass door revealed the garden, showing honeysuckle, huge water butts, and plum and apple trees. Each of the three bedrooms had its own bathroom.

Solicitors, accountants and surveyors were summoned, but I heard nothing more for weeks, indeed months, until one day I made myself say casually to Clive, 'I suppose you've decided not to go ahead with the house at Speen?'

'What do you mean, not go ahead? I take it over next week. I thought you liked it?'

'I do ... I do, it's just that you've said nothing about it for so long.'

'No, as soon as everyone agreed it was a marvellous buy, I went straight ahead. I've just been waiting for all the conveyancing to be got out of the way. We ought to go down next weekend and decide what needs doing.'

So, drugged to the eyebrows, with tape measures, notebooks, pencils and a bottle of brandy to combat the temperature and our colds, we set off. The house had been left curtained and carpeted. I felt we could move in more in more or less there and then, with beds, essential kitchen equipment and comfortable garden furniture which could be used inside or out until we found things we liked. But Clive was against doing this before we'd put in complete central heating. How Billie Birkett survived seven winters there before succumbing, God only knows, but she was a hardy Scandinavian lady, and her skis were still in the garage as witness to those times when she was so snowed in she couldn't drive to the village.

My divorce by now was absolute, but I kept saying, and meaning, I'd never, never marry again. So I used to wonder, while waiting for the builders to finish, what change the house would make in my life and Clive's. I think I thought that each weekend, or whenever we were at Speen, we would be together, and during the week we would each return to our own London nests, me to my studio and Clive to his Weymouth Street flat. During the months of absence from Clive in Dingle, I had plenty of time to think seriously of my life and myself. The fact I established was that I must be prepared to accept my

135

culpability for the ultimate failure of most of the relationships in my life. There was a destructive streak I brought to love affairs which, at certain moments, turned to boredom, carrying in its wake sharp-tongued, put-down criticism. I realized it was a piece of recurring immaturity I had better learn to conquer.

As it happened I didn't have much time to ponder this, because Teddy Joseph, a production manager I'd met on *The Prince and the Showgirl* a lifetime ago, asked if I would see John Schlesinger, who was planning a new film. I said I would like to read the script first so that I knew what we would be talking about, and this duly arrived. On the title page was written *Sunday, Bloody Sunday*, or maybe just 'Bloody Sunday' at that stage, and below it was a name that rang alarm bells, for the line read, 'An original screenplay by Penelope Gilliatt'.

XVIII

I read the script. The story, put simply, was about a triangular love affair between a homosexual doctor, a divorced career woman, and a sexually ambivalent designer with whom they were both in love and who loved them, but neither as much as he loved his career.

John Schlesinger, whom I'd met often with Clive, I like enormously; his total honesty and witty indiscretions are a joy. I went to see him and had no sooner sat down than he said, 'You've worked with x, what do you think of him?' I pulled a face and gave my not complimentary view.

'Well,' said John, 'that's what I think too, but Penelope wants him.'

'Don't let her have him, she doesn't have to work with him. You do.'

That gossipy exchange out of the way, it was clear John was assuming, and rightly, that I wouldn't be seeing him if I didn't want to work with him, and he told me who the key members of the crew were to be, among them Luciana Arrighi as production designer.

As a little girl of six, soon after the war ended, Luciana and her sister Nike had been brought by their mother, Eleanora, from Italy to Sydney to meet their Australian grandparents. Eleanora was an old friend of my sister Pauline and her two daughters were beautifully photographed by Alec at Merioola, identically dressed in muslin and surrounded by ferns on a white rustic iron seat. But it was at around this time that I left Australia for England, and not until the very early sixties did I see any of them again. Luciana, who by then had graduated from the very same prison art school in Sydney that I had been to, visited me in London to find out if there was any chance of working with me. But I needed assistants who were technically more accomplished than myself, and in her case I felt she ought to do either a training course at the BBC, or to be for a while assistant to an inspired fashion designer. In the event she did both, working in Paris with Yves Saint Laurent and after that at the BBC, emerging as a first class designer not only of costumes, but also of sets. Since then, although there's a difference of twenty years between us, we have developed a deep and valuable friendship.

Sunday, Bloody Sunday was produced by Joe Janni, one of the very few truly creative producers it has ever been my good fortune to work with. He has an endearing habit of syntax whereby he starts sentences with the phrase 'In many ways I must tell you ...' When Clive once asked him if he'd ever been to Egypt he said, 'Oh, yes, in many ways I must tell you my grandfather was a close friend of Thomas Cook – he went with him on the first organized tour up the Nile.'

John and Joe were, for the most part, a perfect partnership. They could have furious rows yet remain close friends, and this suited them. I remember hell breaking loose one day, so severely that the entire unit crept away and hid in corners. But John emerged smiling from ear to ear. 'That's better,' he said, 'I knew there was something wrong with this film: Joe and I hadn't had a row.'

John, a wonderfully intelligent man with tremendous flair and inventiveness, veers between great optimism and deep gloom. But even in his moments of despair, he's still capable of sending himself sky high. He had a nervous trick of standing next to Anne Skinner, the continuity girl, unconsciously selecting a strand of her shiny, shoulder-length hair, and winding it tightly round his finger. I never knew how she escaped without looking like Shirley Temple.

The cast was a brilliant one: the three in the love triangle were Glenda Jackson as Alex, Murray Head as the designer, and Peter Finch as the doctor. I had known Peter in Australia when he was a young actor and I an art student. It was an enormous pleasure now to work with him. We would spend hours between takes gossiping about the past.

Glenda Jackson I didn't know, but when she came to my studio to talk about the sort of clothes the character of Alex would wear she was remarkably helpful, and throughout the making of the movie was funny, down-to-earth and articulate.

Rehearsals were in an hotel next to the British Museum. I arrived there very early one morning and neither John nor any actors had arrived, so I thought breakfast, which I hadn't had, would fill the time well. I went into the restaurant and sat down, to be followed seconds later by Penelope Gilliatt. I waved and said, 'Sit with me.' she was very white, thin and shaky, so I started a conversation, any conversation, until she started to relax.... How good I thought her screenplay was.... Did she like living in America? ... How was Nolan, her daughter by John Osborne? Eventually, she calmed down, asked after Clive ... what I'd been doing ... and then, 'Tell me, how is Johnny?' I said, 'Penelope, I don't know, I never see him.' She went a paler shade of white and said, 'I don't believe it ...'

'Nor do I, but nevertheless, it's true.'

We continued this rather unreal conversation until I was able to escape. I would see her occasionally during the rest of the rehearsal time, when I would go in to try something on someone very quickly, but by the time we started shooting, she had returned to New York.

The main location was in a house on Wandsworth Common, where lived, for the purposes of the film, a soppily intellectual trendy couple played by Vivien Pickles and Frank Windsor. In the plot they were going away for the weekend to enjoy some kind of political knees-up, while Glenda and Murray stayed to look after the family pets and the children. The laws governing children working on films are strict, insisting that they are given ample time to rest, to learn with a governess in attendance, and only short bouts of acting. The eldest of the children we'd engaged, Lucy, was delightfully responsible, which had a good effect on the others. The youngest was a baby who looked to me like a featureless bundle of white knitting, but gave an excellent performance crying on cue. One of the two in between was Emma Schlesinger, John's four-year-old niece, who so liked being swung round by her arms that we were all dizzy at the end of each day.

All four were smashing children, real, without a trace of being acting-school monsters. Despite this, we seemed to spend a lifetime in that Wandsworth house. Once we'd finished there, life became easier, and when Easter arrived, with four welcome days off, Clive and I were able to move into the house at Speen. I arranged for everything to be delivered on the Saturday morning, and went down very early in a huge car loaded to the brim with cushions, blankets, towels, cooking pots and food. Cannily, Clive arrived later, by which time all the beds were in place, the dining table and chairs in the dining-room and, because it was such a marvellous day, the furniture in the garden.

For seven years Lady Birkett had been looked after by Winnie Lowes who lived in a tiny cottage nearby and whose grandfather had occupied one of the original brick and flint cottages before anyone had dreamed of joining them together and turning the surrounding land into a garden. Michael Birkett had asked her if she would see me. I wanted to persuade her to work for us, and though I wasn't over-confident I'd succeed, because I knew how devoted she'd been to Billie Birkett, she agreed to come for three days a week and we would both see how we got on.

It didn't take long for us to get on like houses on fire. In the garden, for which we shared a passion, was an enormous cedar tree, and she told me how, as a tiny girl, she had buried a cocoa tin full of silver threepenny bits somewhere under it and had never been able to find the tin again. I was forever full of hopeful extra-sensory perception, and would go out and dig up a couple of feet hoping to be able to present Winnie with her hoard, but I was never able to find it.

After Easter, we started filming night locations, where you begin shooting in the day and carry on until round midnight, catching people entering or leaving houses or restaurants, and doing shots of cars driving through endless streets. Everyone hated this night shooting except me; for some eccentric reason I loved it. The only full night we did was in Piccadilly Circus. There was to be a short scene with Peter Finch being stopped by a drunken piece of rough trade from his past, and then we hoped to pick up with a concealed camera any junkies, pill-poppers or main-liners that we could find.

John arrived very full of electricity and excitement, as always at the beginning of a new scene, looked round his assembled crew and said, 'You, Jocelyn, come with me.' Off we went round the back streets and dark doorways of Piccadilly. A few zonked-out people lurched at us, but as likely from drinking too much as from anything else. On we walked, across Piccadilly Circus, then down a flight of stone steps, me following like Mary's little lamb, without a thought in my head. Suddenly John said, 'I don't think you should come here, darling.' We were in the men's lavatory, with drug addicts, the hypodermics still in their hands, passed out on the grotty floor. I went back, up the stairs, as if the devil had been at my heels. We'd found what we were looking for, but in no way was it filmable.

We finally got the sequence we wanted by contrivance and using our own extras, shooting in an all-night chemist's a few minutes before midnight when all the blank-faced and shaking registered addicts are waiting to get their next day's prescriptions filled. The scene, drained of colour, had as uneasy and bizarre a quality to it as the hideous underground spectacle that shook us so.

When the first light of dawn started to streak the sky, all the equipment was loaded into its various trucks. I took a taxi to Marylebone Station, telephoned Clive, who was at Speen, and asked him to meet the milk train at Great Missenden, which was leaving in a few minutes. It was magic chugging through the early spring light. Once at Great Missenden, we were up the hill to Speen and within ten minutes I was asleep in bed.

As soon as all the outside filming was done we moved to Bray Studios for the interior shooting. It's a nice small studio with a garden running down to the Thames and, like Twickenham, a pleasant, intimate feeling. In our second or third week there, John said to me, 'What on earth are you doing, coming in every day? Your side of things is established for weeks to come. Why aren't you in the country making your new house comfortable?' I unconvincingly muttered, 'You might need me.' 'Nonsense,' he said, 'when I need you you'll be here; off you go.'

Clive had some free time too, so both of us were able to look in all the antique shops between Amersham and Aylesbury and find some surprising bargains. Also, all the furniture I loved but didn't really need in my studio I had moved down to Speen. Quite soon the house was not only furnished, but marvellously comfortable.

I enjoy almost more than anything living for the first year with a new garden, watching it all come to life. There were crocus and miniature daffodils under the trees, pinks and gentian in a small rock garden, and a wide, long herbaceous border crammed full of very special things: a great clump of oriental poppies, a white tree peony, tall bearded iris of such beauty that I could scarcely bring myself to pick them. The house itself was covered in wistaria and creamy white roses. Best of all, in a broad strip across the meadow, were the same wild orchids I had been obliged to walk over in Ireland. Apparently, there is a chalk vein crossing England carrying with it Orchis maculata, and when we eventually sold the house in 1976 these wondrous flowers were what I most minded leaving behind.

For nearly a month at this time Clive and I were alone together at Speen, truly getting to know each other and finding we needed each other, so that, when in London, I moved out of my studio and into his flat in Weymouth Street. As soon as my feelings are engaged, I find it as easy to say, 'I love you,' as to say, 'I'm hungry.' Not so Clive, who is more cautious and who was then more emotionally locked in. But what he didn't know was how much he told me in his sleep. The words he did or didn't say when he was awake weren't important, because every night I had this phantom lover in my bed who poured out his heart to me. On one occasion, when his love and a nightmare became intertwined, he rescued me across seven feet of bed from a burning outhouse, reassuring me that I would be all right, the ambulance was coming, but I must be still and patient. That dream was so dramatic, and he awoke so dazed and uncertain after it, that I told him the bare facts of what I'd gathered of his nightmare while he was talking in his sleep. It wasn't until he was able to say, 'I love you,' with his eyes wide open in the broad light of day that I told him fully about the rich dream life we'd been leading together for months.

When one has looked on the changing face, the appearance, of the same person for nearly twenty years, it becomes difficult adequately to describe those changes unless they have been radical. John Osborne, when I first met him, was a golden-haired, blue-eyed Apollo, a little on the moody side; but when I last saw him he had turned into a benevolent, though recognizable, gentleman of letters. Clive, when I first met him, had short brown hair, a straight nose, dark hazel eyes which smiled easily, a squarish face, and a slim, sculptural body. His body and the quality of the skin remain the same. The skin is smooth and olive and pleasurable to run one's fingers over, like silk. His hair is now like gunmetal in the winter, but two days in the sun turn it into an aureole of sterling silver. He has collected a mass of laughter lines round his eyes and I don't know why I haven't too, because he makes me laugh more than I make him. When he's thinking he frowns, so now, between his eyebrows, are two deep vertical lines. I love to look at him when he's asleep: he has an air of such innocence about him. But the moment he opens his eyes, after the first, almost childlike, loving mumble is out of the way, he becomes a power-house of energy, alert, alive and on the go. For the most part the energy is controlled, but on days when it's not, I go and hide myself in a remote and quiet corner of the house. If his energy level is high once a week, mine is just above average twice a year. He can sustain interest in several projects at once. I like to tackle one thing at a time. Yet we can perfectly happily sit in a room together for hours without either of us doing anything. His great passion is the grandest opera; mine is the garden, and a little chaste chamber music. Over the years, though bits of each of us have flaked off and adhered to the other, we haven't become one whole. We have remained two separate, interacting identities having, I suppose, the miraculous attraction of opposites.

But we first began to understand, truly to know, each other in those early weeks at Speen. They ended when I had to return to Bray for a series of short sequences, using actors we hadn't filmed before, which meant more fittings and more watching how well one costume worked against another. The advantage of working in the theatre, as opposed to films, is that you know every costume will be seen from head to foot, back and front, and also the context in which it will be seen. With films, particularly in interior scenes, the public's view of a person may be limited to just a neckline, a shoulder and an arm, which isn't much good if you've designed a dress with the main interest round the hem. And there is no way of knowing what the camera will shoot until the set-up is composed through the lens.

Oddly, I can't remember the last day of shooting, but I do recall that we were all sad it was over, for it had been a stimulating and happy time. By now I had worked without a break on three films: *Alfred the Great*, *Ryan's Daughter* and *Sunday, Bloody Sunday*. I was tired and a spell of long idle weeks at Speen was all I wanted and all I could think of with pleasure.

But as soon as friends realize you are not so deep in the country as to be inaccessible, they invite themselves to meals or for the weekend. This was something I hadn't been expecting, but soon got used to. We had Dee and Freddie Ayer to stay and Sue and Alec Murray and, as ever, Vangie came whenever she wished. What I couldn't get used to was the sudden attachment to the house of Clive's erstwhile lover, Penelope Mortimer. The first day she came, a collection of Clive's cousins and their children were with us for lunch. It was high summer and we had eaten in the garden. At tea time, Penelope's face peered round the front gate, I think slightly surprised by the number of

143

people. However, she knew everyone and came in. I, full of a graciousness which I didn't feel, suggested Clive show her the garden. During their walk, Clive told me later, she said, 'I would like this house and to get rid of *her*.'

Weekend upon weekend after that she would invite herself down, accompanied by an ill-trained but quite sweet dog, who scared all hell out of my Siamese cats. On Sunday evenings I would sometimes say to Clive, 'What are you doing tomorrow?' And if he had to go up to London and I had decided to stay at Speen, Penelope would stay at Speen too. She was typing like a tornado in the downstairs bedroom, a book later published as *The Home*. I used the upstairs spare room to paint in, and around midday Penelope would appear behind me and watch over my shoulder. To be watched while I'm working is, for me, the worst invasion of privacy, tantamount to rape. I would automatically put down my brushes and ask her if she'd like a drink, anything to remove her prying eyes. I often used to wonder how she'd react if I had gone in to her bedroom and read over her shoulder the page in her typewriter as she typed.

Over lunch she would catechize me. I believe she thought I was possessed of black magic. 'How did you get Clive to ask you to live with him?' I never told her he hadn't. 'How did you get Clive to buy this house? He never offered me anything like this.' By now she had clearly given up all idea of getting rid of me and taking my place. She seemed to realize that whatever had happened wasn't as a result of my manipulation but of Clive's desire for change.

At about this time, quite unexpectedly, Clive's secretary announced she was to be married and would be going to live in South Africa. This left him miserably alone to deal with unsolicited manuscripts, out-of-work actors, and the thousand and one other requests that film directors receive daily by post and telephone. We considered advertising, when I suddenly thought of Sonia McGuinness. She and I had met regularly during the ten years she'd worked for John Osborne, but she'd left him some twelve months before, having astonished herself and her husband, Mac, by discovering she was having another child; she already had a son of seventeen, Jeremy. Now the baby, Adam, was ten months old and Sonia was bored to tears working part-time for a solicitor. Clive didn't need a full-time secretary; someone who could come to his flat in Weymouth Street three days a week would be more than adequate, so it seemed to me a good idea that they should meet. I thought life with us might be more interesting than typing law reports, and so it proved. Very soon Sonia had virtually taken over the running of the household. I have visions of her as a very spry seventy, still organizing our lives, by which time I'll be eighty.

CHAPTER

XIX

One evening Clive and I were at some sort of trendy film party at the Dorchester, and across the room I saw Nat Weiss, the American director of publicity for MGM. He came over and said, 'Hi, Jocelyn, I wanna talk to you about your trip to the States.'

'I'm not going to the States, Nat.'

'Oh yes you are, to promote *Ryan's Daughter.*'

'No, I'm not.'

'Well, at least lunch with me next week.'

'OK,' I said, 'but it won't do any good.'

We met at the Connaught the following Wednesday. Nat Weiss wasn't director of publicity for nothing. Even before we began the meal, he had me nearly crying into my aperitif over the state of the entire British film industry: 'The success of *Ryan's Daughter* in America is vital to the whole movie business in this country, Jocelyn.' In the end, I found myself weakly agreeing to do a three-week whistle-stop tour.

I set out with nothing but dread in my heart. I knew exactly what I was about to undergo: identical questions asked by different people in different accents, day after day. I remembered too that though it was now maxi-skirt time in Europe, the mini was still going strong in America. Women would draw in their breath sharply as I swept into interview after interview with pleats flapping round my ankles. 'You don't expect that to catch on here, do you?' It would be useless to explain the inexorable movements of fashion. I would simply have to reply that inevitably at some time they would suddenly find they wanted to alter the length of their hems, and they would of course sniff as though they knew better. There are, it seems to me, very few American women with any sense of style. They choose a role model (for years it was Jackie Kennedy, when most of them looked like Barbie dolls) and appear to feel uncomfortable if they're not dressed in the same uniform.

New York was my first stop and the only place where I have ever got angry with any journalist. A young girl had been sent by a feminist paper for an interview and she arrived with MGM's traditional press kit under her arm: stills from the film, a précis of the plot, the names of the cast and a list of principal crew members, plus a biography of whomever is going to be interviewed. She flounced in swinging her glossy tresses, and sat down. Question one was: 'Is *Ryan's Daughter* the first film you have ever designed, Miss Rickards?'

'Is this the first interview you've ever conducted?' I snapped back.

Surprised, she said no, she was very experienced.

I asked her why in that case she hadn't done her homework, and she looked as blank as a plank. So I pointed to the MGM file under her arm and said, 'Read that, and when you've digested it, let's start again.'

She was however the only unprepared and unprofessional journalist I met during the whole tour. Some, it's true, were boring, but many were perceptive and intelligent, and in New York I was gratified to come across quite a number of young left-wing writers for whom *Alfred the Great* had become a cult movie, so much so that after ten minutes or so, despite feeling disloyal to Clive, I had to steer them away from that on to *Ryan's Daughter*.

In other ways too my New York stay was enjoyable. Robert Mitchum who, like me, was there promoting *Ryan's Daughter*, turned up with his chic, quick-witted business manager, Reva Frederick, and they asked me over for a drink just as they were settling into the Plaza. When I arrived, they were unpacking and sorting out press kits. So I was given a large tumbler of Jack Daniels and asked to look after myself for a while. As it was the first second I'd had that day in which I could relax, I stretched out on the living room sofa, reflecting that the previous occupant of the suite had been Jerry Lewis. Suddenly my eyes focused on the moulding on the ceiling. I looked, looked again, and to my amazement saw fairly clearly fifteen perfectly formed pats of butter clinging to the rather beautiful baroque plasterwork above our heads. The manager was telephoned, turned not a hair, and had the pats removed with speed and many apologies. But as Mitchum, thinking of his reputation, said to me, 'If you hadn't noticed them, they'd have said that I'd slung them up at their precious ceiling during a drunken spree.'

That night we had dinner together, joined by Trevor Howard and his wife Helen Cherry. We were walking down memory lanes soggy with Dingle's mud, when I looked at the time and cried, 'Jesus, I've got to be on a plane for New Orleans in four hours.' Robert said, 'We'll all come and help you pack,' but I thought it would be quicker and I might even get a couple of hours' sleep if I did it alone. Robert asked me whom I knew in New Orleans and, when I said not a soul, he exploded and said MGM were a lot of idiots to send me by myself. He then, so I was later told, spent twelve hours ringing a friend every hour on the hour until he eventually reached him. The consequence was that after lunch next day a man with a pleasant, soft voice rang me in New Orleans to say that he'd been detailed by Robert Mitchum to take care of me. This he most beautifully did. He drove me all round the city and then beyond it. I saw all I wanted of the architecture, tasted gumbo and ate *pompano* – butterfish – *en papillotte*. I picked some Spanish moss, which trails like mist from the branches of the trees, and was fascinated by the cemetery. 'We have to bury them above ground here,' my new friend told me. 'Below, the ground's too wet and boggy, they'd just float straight out to sea.'

I was staying on the edge of the French Quarter in a marvellous hotel, six storeys high, with beautiful wrought iron balconies all the way round it, a huge revolving mahogany and glass door, and the most efficient and elegantly uniformed porters imaginable. Dressed in short-tail coats, wasp waistcoats, and with a curled yellow ostrich feather on the brims of their shiny black hats, they were, to a man, tall, thin and black, and must have been chosen for their looks.

My suite, too, was of extraordinary elegance. The drawing room had dark green striped walls of satin and damask, and Regency mahogany furniture; good paintings hung from pale green velvet ribbons. The bedroom was huge and light with a white painted bamboo four poster bed. Both rooms were filled with flowers and fruit. For the first time ever I was in an hotel where I didn't have to hide something from sight.

Before Robert Mitchum's friend found me, I had already wandered round the French Quarter, from the 'Streetcar Named Desire' (now kept under shelter as a museum piece) along streets every one of which recalled a song, and every one with houses of vividly painted clear colours and miraculous ironwork, all fronted by verandas supported on slender iron columns. After a walk to the banks of the Mississippi, where a paddle steamer lay at rest, I had returned to the hotel, discovered a long dark oyster bar with sawdust on the floor, ordered a small bottle of Chablis and a dozen oysters, then another dozen, and tottered upstairs to put myself and last night's New York hangover to bed. When Robert's friend arrived, I woke from a blissful sleep feeling almost like a normal human being.

When MGM eventually showed its face some hours later in the form of a personable young man, we worked doing interviews until it was time for us to fly to Atlanta, of which I remember nothing but the monstrous hotel. Its elevators – lifts to me – were made of metal and glass, and travelled up the inside and outside of the building, clinging like insects to the walls. My MGM nanny, the personable young man, told me that the favourite spectator sport in the cocktail lounge, situated in the interior courtyard with a good view of the Hanging Gardens of Babylon, was suicide watching. I was well able to believe him. The plant-bedecked half walls on each floor invited anyone with vertigo, or vertigo plus depression, to jump; and I, who can't stand on a chair without feeling insecure, would scurry from one of the beetle-like elevators to my room clutching at any wall which went all the way up to the ceiling.

Next stop was Dallas, where my driver said he had been chauffeur in the car behind Jack Kennedy's in that last dreadful motorcade. I believed his appalling, gory story. Or were Dallas drivers trained to give Academy Award performances to scare the shit out of visiting Brits?

By now I was getting into my stride with television interviews, and if a question came up that I'd been asked so often I was bored by it, I managed to twist the answer so that I could go off on a riff of my own – albeit about *Ryan's Daughter*. I felt far happier delivering fresh information, rather than replying to old questions with old answers as though I were a performing parrot.

From Dallas I moved to Los Angeles and the rustic charms of the Bel Air Hotel. An artificial stream wandered through the garden, serene swans floated on the lake and all the delicious flowers that grow in hot climates scented the air. I was given a kind of doll's house of my own: large sitting-room, bedroom, bathroom. The weather was perfect, not too hot, and if I left the windows and the front door open it was even cool enough to justify lighting the huge log fire. Happily, I was also amongst friends again, those I'd made working on films. Jane Sprague showed me Los Angeles as she had shown me Rome all those years before, and on the rare occasions when I had nothing to do I would go out of the back gate of the hotel to look at the most magical tree I have ever seen. Immensely high, with a shiny grey trunk and blossoms on its branches like rose pink cattleya orchids, it should have been the tree from which Eve picked the fruit. Not long ago I noticed that someone with sense has planted a whole row of them beside the Ahmansson Theatre at the downtown Music Center.

In Los Angeles there was a change of nannies; this time I was in the care of the altogether admirable Regina Gruss. My first appointment was at a television station in Orange County, where I was driven in a limo only slightly longer than the Duke of Wellington's iron hearse, and taken into a monster studio where several shows were clearly being taped at once. How this was done without everyone picking up a jumbled sound-track is still a mystery to me.

As far as I remember, we were going out live on Breakfast Television. I was sharing the programme with four nubile bell ringers and Buckminster Fuller, who even then was an old man and deaf as a post. While we were waiting, and not wishing to add to the noise level, I fished round for a pen and a piece of paper, wrote on it 'I'm a great fan of yours', and passed it to him. He then fished about in his pockets, found a card which he signed 'Sincerely, Buckminster Fuller', and passed it to me. This friendly but mute exchange was at the time when he wanted to control weather by erecting giant domes over cities, so I put on the back of his card, 'I've always wanted a dome of my own'. He returned this with, 'They come more expensive than autographs!' – at which we both got the giggles and had to cease communication. But after I had done my bit for *Ryan's Daughter* I stayed behind to hear his interview. There were so many questions I wanted to ask him that I longed to be in the interviewer's chair myself, and to my dismay these questions were never put, partly I believe because television interviewers stick closer to prepared scripts than other journalists. It's as though they've lost the ability to think on their feet.

Among all the interviews I did with newspapers, the one I most enjoyed was with a bright young man, Alan Cartnal, on the *Los Angeles Times*, whose first words to me were a blunt, 'You smoke too much.' I agreed – forty a day had been my ration for God knows how long – but said he should take into account exceptional circumstances: I was having to perform eighteen hours a day. 'I'm giving up when I'm home,' I said. At the time this was only half meant; but as it happened, my first act on getting back to London was to burn every cigarette I was carrying and I have never smoked again.

My worst ordeal was a press conference at the MGM studios in Los Angeles with suburban newspaper fashion editors. They didn't really know what questions to ask to draw out interesting answers. They found my job – designing for characters in a film so that their clothes reveal their personalities – utterly alien. I was forced to do a sort of spontaneous cabaret. I just hope they got something out of it.

As I was leaving MGM on that occasion I ran into Norman Savage, David Lean's editor, who put his head into the car and said, 'Do you want to come and see a cut sequence?' I was into the viewing theatre in a second, and although I had seen all the rushes of *Ryan's Daughter*, I was in no way prepared for the impact of a properly edited part of it. He let me out three quarters of an hour later, with tears streaming down my face, and I had to re-do my entire make-up in the back of the car on the way to yet another television interview.

Then, at last, a weekend off. I stayed in bed most of the Saturday feeling as though I'd been put through the mangle, but on the Sunday Norman Savage and his wife came for a drink bringing David Lean and Sandy, whom I hadn't seen since Dingle. So we spent several happy hours swapping the gossip from all our varied encounters from one end of the States to the other. When David and Sandy left, Jane Sprague, who had been with me for most of the weekend, remarked, 'You never said David was as attractive as that.'

On the Monday evening with – can you believe – a third change of nanny, Judson Moses, I was on the move once more, from Los Angeles to Cleveland, Ohio. By now jet lag was catching up with me. But I had to be fairly fresh for a breakfast interview next morning, so on arrival I went straight to bed.

At the interview, as well as the journalist, there was a tiny little old lady like a frail-boned bird, but sharp as a tack, to whom, as the owner of every cinema in the area, much deference was paid. The usual television appearances followed. But in the evening Jud and I set off again, this time for Detroit, in which city it's easy to believe that babies will soon be born with tiny wheels instead of feet. Wherever you look there are cars, or rather automobiles, stretched away endlessly into infinity over huge flat expanses. I found the whole place so horrendous that my only memory is of being placed in a glass booth like a coffin set bang in the middle of a busy shopping centre. Here I was interviewed by a man with a telephone, and when we'd finished, and suffered through several commercials which he delivered with a painfully false vitality, he requested that listeners phone in questions to me. I think I only fielded three or four calls; few of them were interesting, and none of my replies was even remotely illuminating.

With this particular horror over, it was not long, thank God, before I was put on a plane for home by Jud, whom I now loved as a brother. I extended the foot rest of my front seat, lay back with a jumbo Jack Daniels in my hand, consumed a huge plate of ice cream so the air hostess would stop worrying because I was too tired to eat, and flaked out until the plane was over London.

As soon as it had landed, I was out into the main concourse and in Clive's arms like a homing pigeon. We drove to Speen and there blissfully I breathed in the country air, the scent from the garden, and the apple and cherry wood burning in the fireplace.

It was some days before I realized just how exhausting my twenty-one day publicity jaunt had been. I wonder if anyone has ever been persuaded to do that sort of thing twice. I imagine not, or if so they are gluttons for punishment. From something like the fifth day on, you are fighting all your inner time clocks; all your usual devices against boredom run out. You drop into bed exhausted and wake up in the morning tired. Yet you must still stay on top of everything because a slip of the tongue, or an over-honest word, is going to land you and the film company up to your collective necks in trouble. The only compensation is that once you are back home and rested, the press cuttings start arriving and the very flattering letters of thanks. So the horrors fade and you merely feel relief that you've at least survived, and done it all as best you can.

However, rested or not, it seemed to be taking me a long time to recover my normal energy. I looked hideously puffy and felt constantly slightly sick, almost as though I were pregnant, which I knew I was not. Clive was extremely worried and eventually Alec Murray said, 'For God's sake get her to go to a decent doctor. She's been diagnosing and prescribing for herself for years.' Clive immediately took me to his doctor, who was a diagnostic magician. After examining me, he said, 'It's your gall bladder and I don't think it's gall stones. Off you go to St George's Hospital, where there's a genius who will take special x-rays.'

I spent most of a day at St George's, arriving early and having, as instructed, eaten nothing since six o'clock the evening before. The genius x-rayed away until lunchtime, then told me to go out, eat the richest lunch I could find, return and have more x-rays. At the end, he showed me the endless collection of huge and horrible photographs of my gall bladder which he was sending on to the surgeon to whom I later presented myself, Sir Rodney Smith, a tall, quiet man with the only form of bedside manner I trust, total directness. 'It'll have to come out,' he said. 'I won't know what's wrong with it until I open you up.'

I was duly operated on and when he came to see me afterwards he said, 'No wonder you were feeling rotten. Under the anaesthetic we couldn't even manipulate it properly with the pressure of our hands. One of the two ducts was totally blocked. You'll feel much better without it.' He was right. I'd gone under the anaesthetic feeling ghastly and come round feeling a bit tender, but miraculously better.

That spring and early summer of 1971 were spent happily at Speen, just relaxing and enjoying feeling well. I had now totally lost interest in designing, as though it were a vein of gold bearing ore which I'd completely exhausted, and I had once more turned seriously to painting.

Clive and Michael Birkett had both been asked to join the council for the Venice Film Festival, so Junia Birkett and I decided to go too.

I hadn't been to Venice before, but it was love at first sight once we had left the terminal and were in our *motoscafo*. Along the watery road of the Grand Canal it was siesta time, so all was comparatively calm; and I at least knew what I was passing, having digested Mary McCarthy's *Venice Observed* and James Morris's *Venice*. (Incidentally, I don't think Jan Morris writes nearly as well as James Morris.) On the right, under the Rialto Bridge, I saw the Rezzonica, and no leap of the imagination could make me feel that Elizabeth Barrett, Robert Browning and their sickly child had felt at home there – certainly not as much at home as I would be, I thought. Then came the Accademia, which I knew was crammed to overflowing with paintings I longed to see. On the other side, the Piazza San Marco revealed only a fraction of its perfect scale. Another quick turn of the head, but all I could glimpse of Peggy Guggenheim's palazzo was the plain high white wall. Gradually we approached the Lido and the Hotel Excelsior, and beside it – shades of *Death in Venice* – the Hotel des Bains.

Our room at the Excelsior on the top floor had a huge terrace, looking in one direction over the lagoon and in the other, the Adriatic. It was a perfect vantage point from which to watch the change of light on the water. I didn't wish that I were Canaletto or Guardi, but rather the old Turner, who surely knew better than any other painter how to extract the maximum dazzling display of sun or moon on sea and sky.

The most beautiful American boy I have ever seen was staying alone in the hotel. He turned out to be the Reynald's tobacco heir. I would get pleasure simply from sitting and looking at him; he was like a sun burned youth from a Botticelli painting, with sun-streaked blond hair to his shoulders and clear, aquamarine eyes. I used to think, as we made friends with him, that there should be some way of preserving such exquisite beauty so that it remained the same forever, a work of art. He was like a piece of fruit at the very peak of perfection and one didn't want him to age by even an hour. Alas and inevitably, the next time I saw him, not very long afterwards, he was just another good-looking young man like many others, and no longer my own particular Tadzio with strange echoes of *Death in Venice*.

Sunday, Bloody Sunday was one of the films in competition at the Festival, so Joe and Stella Janni were at the Excelsior, as were John Schlesinger with the photographer Michael Childers, and Glenda Jackson and her husband. It was like London-on-Adriatic. Sitting one day having a drink with Michael Balcon and Aileen, his wife, I took my courage in both hands and said to him, 'Actually, you know, you and I have met before, but perhaps you don't remember?' My heart was a little in my mouth because this was when he and I had exchanged high words over the casting of Joan Plowright in *The Entertainer*. But he put back his head and roared with laughter, saying, 'How could I forget such a chit of a girl telling me I didn't know my own job. I've forgiven you now.'

In the luminous light of the first evening, Michael, Junia, Clive and

I had left the Lido and gone to dinner in Venice. I remember that travelling there across the water was like being encapsulated in a moonstone; and when we disembarked at the Piazza San Marco I noticed that its scale seemed to create a kind of optical illusion: no matter where people stand, their heads appear to be on the same plane, unless they are all kaleidoscopically broken up by the flight of pigeons.

One mysterious vision from that first evening I still vividly remember. After dinner at the Fenice Restaurant, next door to the opera house, we had made our way under a rising moon towards the Accademia Bridge through a small, totally deserted and soundless classical square. Suddenly the door of a palazzo was opened and the light streamed out onto the paving stones. Through the door came a tall Venetian beauty in evening dress, followed by between twenty and thirty highly-bred cats. She cooed softly at them as though they were doves, and together she and they did a tour of the square. This ritual completed, the beauty, cooing for the tardier cats, returned through the door and shut it. No more light on the paving stones, nothing but the awareness of the absence of a vision which had been like a glimpse of an illustration to a fairy story.

Most days were were so dreadfully hot that we all ate together at the Excelsior rather than go out into the midday sun. They had – maybe have now – a covered, outside restaurant, separated from the sea and sand by plants, and there I nearly always had my favourite tomato salad lunch. Michael Birkett still often teases me about my love of basil and *rugghetta*, but once the waiters had grown accustomed to my daily requests, I would get enough of both of them to satisfy even me.

We were lunching there as usual one Sunday when I looked up and saw Nelo Risi in the distance. I went over and placed my hands on his shoulders. He spun round and gave me a hug. '*Merde*, I've done it again,' he said. 'I knew you'd designed *Sunday, Bloody Sunday*, but I didn't expect to see you here.' This was a repetition of his greeting at Cannes after the screening of *Blow-Up*. I told him the film wasn't the reason I was in Venice, and pointed back at Clive. 'That man is part of my life, that's why I'm here.' He nodded sagely and said, '*Oui – c'est ton type.*' *Mon type* came over and they instantly liked each other.

I saw Nelo again only briefly during the Festival, but had a really long talk with him when we met later in London, and another later still in Rome. We both to this day like to know where we can find each other at a moment's notice.

That Sunday afternoon Clive and I, with a few friends who included Joe and Stella, Glenda and her husband, Michael Childers and John, took a boat and went to Torcello. On the way we stopped at a tiny island with a Franciscan monastery on it, which Joe had once used as a location for his film of *Romeo and Juliet*. We were shown the refectory and the cloisters. Everywhere we went there were birds – golden pheasants, peacocks, herons, flamingos and ducks – walking round as tame and docile as tortoises. Joe told us that, while he had been there during the shooting, he had eventually succeeded in getting a vital call through to Los Angeles on the one and only island telephone, and as he started to talk, a monk came rushing out, his finger to his lips, saying urgently, 'Shush . . . shush . . . shush,' miming the turning of the camera – a perfect example of how even the most unlikely people, when brought into contact with filming, quickly become totally involved, in this case to the extent of silencing the producer.

At Torcello, the cathedral took my breath away. Considering its age, predominantly eleventh and twelfth century, it is in an amazing state of preservation. The mosaics seem a mystic revelation. In the apse there is one of Mary dressed in the blues of many different skies against a hallucinatory gold background, huge and very simple. At the end, where one now enters, there is another, divided horizontally into a vast fragmented vision of The Last Judgement, taking up the entire wall. I found the cathedral, indeed the whole island, both mysterious and peaceful, and I understood why Torcello is called 'the pearl of the lagoon'.

We dined splendidly at the Taverna Cipriani, loitering over every mouthful, and round about eleven-thirty left to travel back to the Lido by the light of the fullest, most magnificent moon I have ever seen. I spent the short voyage gulping in the visual sensations as though I were frightened of missing something. We were leaving next morning and I was determined to remember everything just in case I didn't return. As we drew level with the Piazzo San Marco, the first strokes of midnight were ringing out, so it seemed only proper to pause there and have a last drink at Florian's. Then we climbed back into our boat and were all too soon at the Excelsior, where I went onto the terrace to have a last look at the moon, my head spinning with memories.

XX

Once home in London I pretended for a while, unsuccessfully, to be a continuing convalescent. Clive, though, was working hard. There came an absurdly crowded morning when not only was he auditioning an actor in the living-room with three others sitting on chairs in the hall waiting their turn, but Kitty McGinty, my old Irish housekeeper, was cleaning the bathroom, Sonia was typing in the kitchen, and I was in bed, with Vangie and Rebecca Breed, the wardrobe mistress from *Blow-Up*, sitting on my feet. Suddenly it was all too much. I leaped out of bed, into the bath, into my clothes, rushed in to Sonia and said, 'Tell Clive I've gone out to lunch with Vangie and Rebecca, and I'll come back when we have somewhere larger to live.'

Later that evening, as Clive and I were having a drink together, he asked if I had really meant what I had said to Sonia. Did I really want a larger house in town?

He well understood my problem. I had no spare room in London in which to do any painting. Every day I felt bursting with energy for work, yet my studio was let to an interior decorator who threatened court action if I tried to get him out. It's true I could have worked at Speen, but if Clive were filming and not there that wasn't practical. My answer to his question was therefore yes, I did think it was a good idea at least to start looking.

Agents were contacted, lists by the score arrived with every post. Of the first batch, several places seemed worth looking at and we made appointments to see them on Clive's first free day. Vangie came too. Our first stop was Eldon Road, off Victoria Road. I had high hopes. It's a very pretty street full of charming houses, and the one advertised

157

had not one single studio, but two. We arrived and it was the only truly hideous building there. We went in out of curiosity, but saw only a rabbit warren of small useless rooms and lots of little staircases that looked as though they belonged in Mole's house in *The Wind in the Willows*.

The second house, viewed after lunch, was in Hamilton Terrace. A man from Chesterton's met us outside a neo-Georgian, red brick beast. My spirits sank. He said, with awe, that it belonged to Lord and Lady Harewood, and my spirits sank further. Lady Harewood I had known in Sydney, first when she was Miss Bambi Tuckwell, violinist with the Sydney Symphony Orchestra, and as beautiful and gentle looking as the little Disney creature she was nicknamed after, and later when she was a model for Athol Shmith, the Melbourne fashion photographer whom she married.

As we entered Vangie and I said, as one, 'Oh, no!' There's no justification for putting wallpaper over windows. The entrance hall, papered I think in a fairly dark green, had absolutely no source of daylight. The Chesterton's man tried hard. 'It's because of Lord Harewood's pictures, you see. He liked them all individually lit.' We went from gloomy room to gloomy room saying, 'My God, how could they have lived in it?' At one point, when looking at the master bedroom, our fascinated attention was drawn to the fur cupboards which were not only cedar-lined – sensible: moths don't like it – but specially wired direct to Scotland Yard. At last the man from Chesterton's said, 'The music room looks onto the garden,' his voice rising with faint hope. We descended via a mingy staircase, and through the glass door leading to the garden we did indeed catch a faint glimpse of autumn. But all the windows were about eye height. That was the last straw.

We bitched a little more and went out into Hamilton Terrace. The man from Chesterton's turned politely to us and said, 'Excuse me, it was impossible for me not to overhear your conversation, but I've learned from it what you're really looking for. There's a house well worth your seeing and about to come on the market about three minutes' walk away. 'Not neo-Georgian, a real period house?' I asked. He nodded and explained that an architect and builders were already at work improving it, and that it was one of the few freehold houses in the area. By this time we were there.

He opened a gate, we walked down a short narrow covered alley, and turned left into a garden which ran along the front of the house

158

and a little beyond it, bringing back all my childhood memories of
The Secret Garden. The house itself was Regency, old London brick
recently re-pointed, and three storeys high if you counted neither the
attic nor the small cellar. We trooped in, this time all going separate
ways, Clive looking for a study, I first searching out a room with a
north light, then rambling everywhere, and finally out again into the
walled garden which even had a miniature wood at the end. Vangie
found me sitting on a rock.

'What are you doing there?' she said.

'Waiting for however long it takes to find out if we can get it. It's
mine and I want it.'

She sat down beside me and we agreed that for us it was the perfect
town house, not very different from one in the country, and there
wasn't any point in looking further until Clive and I knew if we could
afford it.

I made the man from Chesterton's promise not to show it to anyone
else. Clive had a meeting the following day with his solicitor and
accountant, and came back to Weymouth Street smiling. The answer
was, 'Yes – subject to survey', and we had, rightly as it turned out, few
doubts about that being satisfactory with the amount of work
already going on there.

Full of excitement, we made lists of what things we needed
immediately. Then, what about carpets? Siamese cat colour, brown
up the stairs and in most of the rooms, just not quite white in the
bedroom, dressing-room and bathroom, none in my studio; no curtains either – it was to be stripped for action. What about the other
window curtains? White linen blinds, and course, hand-woven
whitish Indian cotton lace. White walls everywhere, except for the
top floor bathroom which needed cheering up. No matter what stage
the builders had reached, we planned to move in within three months,
in February, on the principle that they finish faster if you're standing
over them like a bad fairy. In the event, it worked, and we did.

But now it was early winter, when at Speen the witching hour is the
few minutes when the light is dimming but you can still see from the
house the details in the garden. Every evening at this moment a pro-
cession would move in front of the larches, across a little open space,
and into the hidden area of the vegetable garden. Always in the same
order they came: a doe followed by her fawn, following a long way
behind by a golden cock pheasant with a limp. I never turned the

lights on until they had vanished. One evening that November Clive and I were sitting at the window waiting for them when he said, 'Do you still feel the same way about marriage?'

'Are you proposing to me?'

'Well, yes, I suppose I must be.'

'When? When?' I asked. I clearly didn't still feel the same way about marriage.

We had to go up to London later in the week, returning for the weekend, so on our way through High Wycombe we stopped at the Registry Office and got a special licence to be married there at midday on the Monday. We rang Alec and Sue, Michael and Junia Birkett and Vangie, asking them to be with us then if they could; if not, to meet us at The Bell at Aston Clinton for lunch afterwards. Everyone sounded just as pleased as we felt ourselves, and Junia kept saying, 'I truly never believed you'd get round to it.'

Monday dawned misty but sunny. Clive said, 'What are you going to wear?' I thought for a minute and said, 'Your Moroccan djellabah; what are you?'

'A suit with a polo-necked pullover.'

I got out of bed, collected the breakfast tray, and went down to see Winnie, who was in the kitchen. We talked about the weekend and whether or not we'd get the fog that was, so we'd heard, disrupting London. Before I went back upstairs I said, 'Later this morning, we're going down to High Wycombe Registry Office to get married.' She beamed and said, 'Oh, you'll feel so much better!' *Than what?* I longed to ask her, but didn't, and she told me that's where she'd been married thirty-seven years before. As Clive and I were leaving the house she came running after us saying, 'Is there any film in the camera?' and using an instamatic she took one photograph of us, two small figures against the larches and the misty valley with, in the foreground, long shadows cast by the low winter sun crossing the frosty lawn.

We went for a little drive on our way to High Wycombe, not wishing to appear over-eager. When we got there, the Birketts had already arrived, but they'd only had to drive from the Chalfonts. Michael said the weather report had announced that the fog in London was impenetrable: Alec, Sue and Vangie were clearly delayed, so we didn't wait, and were married in a minute. Alec and I are sadly fated not to witness each other's weddings. We left a loving message, and a map showing the way to The Bell, and went off for our celebration lunch.

We'd no sooner sat down to have a drink than they came in. Vangie had sat up half the night cutting out tissue paper rose petals, and tinting the edges pink; she showered them over me, and I didn't turn a hair, except with pleasure.

We'd thought we'd just go in to the restaurant and say what we wanted to eat as usual. But oh, no, the marvellous and impeccable Michael had ordered everything in advance. We didn't have to stir our minds even to think of that. It was the nicest wedding I'd ever been to. And now, seventeen years later, it is still the nicest wedding I've ever been to. And the only marriage I believe I ever truly made.

161

INDEX

162

McGill, Donald 88
McGill, Kathie 41
McGinty, Kitty 157
McGrath, Joe 104, 107, 108
McGuinness, Adam 144
McGuinness, Frank ('Mac') 77, 144
McGuiness, Jeremy 144
McGuiness, Sonia 71, 76, 77, 144, 145, 157
McIndoe, Sir Archibald 39
McKellen, Ian 116
MacLaine, Shirley 104, 106–9
Maclean, Donald 32
McMillan, Kenneth 60
McNaughton, Bunty 26
McPherson, Kenneth 46, 47, 59
Mademoiselle (Jean Genet) 83, 87, 89, 90, 91, 92, 93, 94
Magic Christian, The 127
Magritte, René 33
ss *Maloja* 2, 59
Manchester 58, 59
Mankowitz, Wolf 56, 57
Maple, Gracie (Gracie Weighall) 23, 24
Marché St Pierre 107
Marcus Aurelius 39
Marina Grande, Capri 63
Marlborough House 123
Marseilles 3
Martin Millicent 56
Mary (Cranley Gardens) 19
Marylebone Station 141
Maugham, Syrie 73
Meals on Wheels (Charles Wood) 88
Medici Gallery 26, 28
Medworth, Frank 13
Melbourne 1, 4, 5, 6, 11, 13, 19, 48, 158
Melbourne Girls' Grammar School (Merton Hall) 5, 12
Mercer David 85
Merchant Vivien 116
Merioola 17, 21, 23, 102, 137
Merioola Group 21
Metro-Goldwyn-Mayer (MGM) 96,

101, 102, 113, 125, 146, 147, 148, 149, 151
Mexico 36
Michelangelo 39
Midsummer Night's Dream, A (Shakespeare) 60
Miles, Sarah 125, 128, 129, 130, 132, 133
Miller, Arthur 52
Miller, Harry Tatlock 19, 20, 21, 23, 24, 41
Miller, Lee 33
Mills, John 126, 134
Mills Paul 113
Milt (MGM, New York) 103
Minton, John 32, 33
Mississippi River 149
Miss World contest 109
Mitchum, Robert 125, 128, 132, 147, 148
Monroe, Marilyn 50, 51, 52
Monsieur le Coq 112
Monte Carlo 41
Moore, Myrtle Pretoria ('Nannie', 'Nurnie') 1
Moorhouse, Maria *see* Marian Cummings
Moreau, Jeanne 85, 87, 88, 89, 90, 91, 92
Morecambe, Lancs. 65, 66
Morecambe Bay 66
Morecambe Palais de Danse 66, 67
Moreton-Evans, Ginette (Ginette Darwin) 80, 105
Morgan, A Suitable Case for Treatment (David Mercer) 85, 87, 90, 104
Morris, James 153
Morris, Jan 153
Morris, Oswald ('Ossie') 66
Mortimer, Penelope 117, 118, 143, 144
Moscow 36
Moses, Judson 151, 152
Mossy (Jocelyn Rickards's driver) 131
Mostel, Zero 112